For years, I have sat in the pew Sunday after Sunday and thought to myself, "Wow! What a good and relevant sermon!" Nevertheless, all of these hundreds of Sunday sermons have not made me a disciple in everyday life! Shocking, but true!
   —Dorte

When I read "The Last Reformation," it became clear to me how the current state of the church happened and why there are so few real disciples in our country. The book reveals facts that most Christians are unaware of about the unbiblical traditions we have ignorantly accepted into the church. How far away from true Christianity we have come.
   —Ulla

This book is credible, and hugely engaging. Torben is very transparent and extremely honest in sharing the difficulties of his own journey toward returning to the biblical way of making disciples, the way Jesus intended. The message is clear, concise, and biblical.
   —Klaus

Torben's book is a must read for anyone who has become dissatisfied with the way church is happening today in many parts of the world. Its pyramid system of leadership closes the door to all but a select few while everyone else pays their tithes into the storehouse, then sits and listens obediently. The abuses and control tactics (to keep us and our money), and the watered-down messages to please the "seekers" must change if we are to become the vibrant and powerful disciples who are carrying on His work and making disciples in all the nations, as Jesus charged us with doing. Let the reformation begin!
   —Eileen

OTHER PUBLICATIONS BY
TORBEN SØNDERGAARD:

"Sound Doctrine"

"Christian, Disciple, or Slave"

"Life as a Christian"

"Complete the Race"

"Deceived?" (Booklet)

"The Twisted Race" (Booklet)

THE LAST REFORMATION

Back to the New Testament model of discipleship

by Torben Søndergaard

THE LAST REFORMATION

Back to the New Testament model of discipleship

By Torben Søndergaard

Paperback: ISBN: 978-1-938526-42-8

ePub (iPad, Nook): ISBN: 978-1-938526-43-5

Mobi (Kindle): ISBN: 978-1-938526-44-2

PUBLISHED BY LAURUS BOOKS

PUBLISHED IN THE UNITED STATES OF AMERICA

LAURUS BOOKS
P. O. Box 894
Locust Grove, GA 30248 USA
www.TheLaurusCompany.com

This book may be purchased in paperback from www.TheLaurusCompany.com and other retailers around the world. Also available in eBook format for electronic readers from their respective stores.

ACKNOWLEDGEMENTS

Thanks to
Sam Blakeley, John van Wendel de Joode,
Scott Galbraith, Ronald Gabrielsen, and others who have
helped to get this book published in English.
You are a blessing.

— Torben Søndergaard

BEFORE YOU BEGIN ...

Throughout this book, the words "fellowship" and "church" are used as having two different meanings.

The word "fellowship" is used primarily for a gathering of believers who have no formal church building or structure and are led exclusively by the Holy Spirit and the Word of God.

The word "church," when used of a gathering, refers to traditional "organized religion," with a formal church building, assigned leadership structure, a congregation of listeners, etc.

Simply said, a "church" is with a building, and a "fellowship" is without a building. It does not always work out that way, but the context will make the meaning clear.

In the same way, if a reference to church does not say "state church," it is referring primarily to evangelical or "free" churches.

References to the "West" or "Western churches" are referring to both European and American churches.

Bible quotations are from the *Modern King James Version* of the Bible.

From the publisher:
Torben Søndergaard, the author of this book, lives in Denmark. This book has been translated from the Danish language into English and contains many references to Denmark as well as the Lutheran Church, which is the "state church" in Denmark.

TABLE OF CONTENTS

INTRODUCTION

We have had the chance to get to know Torben Søndergaard and see him in action. What we have seen is God's kingdom being preached, people being saved, set free, healed, baptized, and filled with the Holy Spirit the way we read about in Acts —and the way it even happens today in many countries and many places where the gospel is being preached in the power of the Spirit.

Torben has a passion for the salvation of people and for the fellowship. People who get saved are quickly introduced into an active discipleship program and into varying fellowships. New Christians quickly begin practicing Jesus' life in word and deed, which in turn leads to others coming to faith in Him.

Torben has studied church history and the Bible, especially Acts, in order to find biblical principles that are applicable to reaching out to people. In this book, he describes his own journey, from which we can all learn something. The training of disciples is a subject that is in focus throughout the whole book, and Torben shows by many examples how we can best train disciples.

Most Christians, us included, have inherited a way to have fellowship and be disciples. Torben challenges us to question this, using examples from the Bible and from church history. This book is challenging and sharp, but we all want to see more people believing in Jesus, disciples being trained and fellowships growing stronger and multiplying. This is why we believe *The Last Reformation* is important when thinking about how we are to be the church today.

We want to encourage you to read this book prayerfully and with an open heart and mind. How you apply what you learn from this book is up to you.

We are truly in need of a paradigm shift in regard to fellowships and discipleship—a Christian lifestyle that reflects what we read in Acts. We believe that it can happen in each country and in our age today!

For God's kingdom and for people's salvation!

— Charles Kridiotis and Mattias Nordenberg

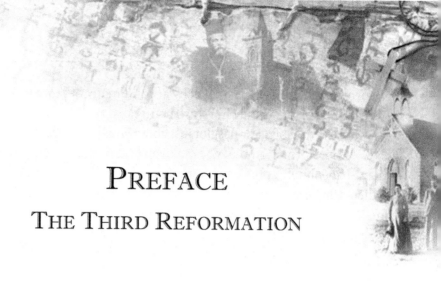

PREFACE

THE THIRD REFORMATION

A German researcher, Christian Schwarz, looking into church growth, says that many things are indicating that we are living in a time when we are going to see a third reformation.

The first reformation took place in the fifteenth century when Martin Luther opposed the Catholic Church and its teaching. He revived the very essence of the Gospel, namely justification by faith alone. One might say that this reformation concerned theology. If you look at the structure of the Lutheran Church today, which is the "state church" in Denmark, you will see that it resembles the structure of the Catholic Church to a great extent. This is because Martin Luther did not introduce very much change to the structure itself.

The second reformation took place in the eighteenth century around the time of the ministry of the Wesley brothers' activities. In this reformation, personal intimacy with Christ was rediscovered. This was mainly a spiritual reformation; a reformation in which the passionate love for one's personal Savior was cherished. It resulted in a passion for missions and evangelism. However, once again, the structure itself— the framework of the church and the service—did not change very much. It was, again, like putting a new patch on old clothes.

If you look back through history, you will see that none of the revivals of the past have seriously done anything about the church structure. What we really need is a new and radical reformation, a third reformation that, as Christian Schwarz and many others think, is going to transform our whole church structure.

The third reformation is not just about small changes here and there. No, it is a reformation that goes so deep that it requires a complete new start. I absolutely agree with Christian Schwarz, Wolfgang Simson, and others who speak out on this subject. What I am about to present in this book is definitely not just my own opinion. Many good books have already been written about this topic, but a large number of them go into such depth that the reader needs a special interest in church history and its structure in order to be able to read them. If that background and training are lacking, then it might be a little difficult to go through them. Therefore, I will not be going into such depths in this book as many others have done. Instead, I want to give the reader a taste of what God is going to do, a taste of the future of the church. Although I am not presenting anything new, it will still be new to most people. It seems that this message has not yet had as much of a breakthrough in Scandinavia and Europe as it has in many other places in the world. I hope, therefore, that this book will help to start a reformation in you, the reader, and that after reading it, you will start to examine the Bible more deeply for yourself to see what it has to say about these things.

I know God wants something new to happen. I also know that this reformation is necessary. Yet, despite the fact that I am so absolutely convinced about the things I am writing, I am still writing it with great fear and trembling because I know this will not be easily accepted.

We are all still glad today for the reformation that Martin Luther introduced. Yes, after five hundred years, we think how fantastic that Reformation was and have an almost idyllic understanding of what really happened. We imagine how Luther stood by the church in Wittenberg on October 31, 1517, and quietly and peacefully nailed his *Ninety-Five Theses* to the door while people were standing behind him applauding. Yes, it was beautiful, and it laid the foundation for the Reformation, which we are happy for today.

We forget about many things, however. We forget that this reformation was not accepted so easily. It created great opposition, resulting in Luther's books being burned and him being accused of having been sent by the devil to wage war with God's church. We forget that it led to violent fights in which thousands of men, women, and children were killed. We forget that the church of that time did not want the reformation, and they did everything to fight it. You might be thinking now: *Yes, but that was the Catholic Church.* Here is my response: *Yes, it was the Catholic Church, but it was still the church.* Today, another church denomination will try to fight what God wants. Why do we think it will be any different today? I am not saying that we will see thousands killed, but why should we think that everything will go smoothly, without divisions, and without being accused of working against God and trying to destroy the church?

The truth is, we need to see this reformation, and it is not going to go smoothly! We are going to be accused of destroying the church. We are going to experience the opposition of many Christians who will be against what we are aiming at. We are going to be accused of having been deceived and of being dangerous. We know, however, that what we are doing is for the church and for God because we have seen something that God wants to happen.

Why did the church turn against Martin Luther? Was it because his words were opposed to the Word of God? No, that was not the reason. For the church, it was not a matter of what the Bible said, but of something completely different. Martin Luther's teaching opposed a system based on finances, power, and control. We can say that this is also relevant today. People will oppose it today as well, not because it is unbiblical, but because it will destroy the system they have helped to build. Finances, power, and control still matter a lot to the church leaders today. This is not because pastors do not want to serve God and do not want to do the right thing. It is mostly due to the fact that they either cannot see it or that they have much to lose that makes it hard for them to go in this direction. When they see others abandoning their system, they will fight it because that is how they lose their members and, together with them, the money that keeps the system running. We will look at this more closely in this book.

Let's read what Jesus did and said:

Now the Passover of the Jews was at hand, and Jesus went up to Jerusalem. And He found in the temple those who sold oxen and sheep and doves, and the moneychangers doing business. When He had made a whip of cords, He drove them all out of the temple, with the sheep and the oxen, and poured out the changers' money and overturned the tables. And He said to those who sold doves, "Take these things away! Do not make My Father's house a house of merchandise!" Then His disciples remembered that it was written, "Zeal for Your house has eaten Me up." (John 2:13-17)

God does not live in a temple built of stone. He lives in us—Christians, His disciples. However, if Jesus walked upon the earth today and saw what was happening, He would react in the very same way. He would not sit back, like we do, and tolerate it.

"Do you suppose that I came to give peace on earth? I tell you, not at all, but rather division. For from now on five in one house will be divided: three against two, and two against three. Father will be divided against son and son against father, mother against daughter and daughter against mother, mother-in-law against her daughter-in-law and daughter-in-law against her mother-in-law ... Yes, and why, even of yourselves, do you not judge what is right?" (Luke 12:51-53, 57)

Jesus is zealous for God's church on earth. Do we have the same zeal today? Jesus said there would be a price to pay if we followed Him. Are we willing to pay that price? It will cause division, and some Christians will fight it because it seems to be something that will destroy the church. I can honestly say on my behalf that I have absolutely no intent of destroying God's church by publishing this book. I am not doing this because I am against the church. I love the church, and, because of that love, I want to rescue it. I love God's people, and I love God, and that is why I do what I do. The only difference is that my view of what God intended His church to be is different from that of many other people.

After the Reformation with Martin Luther, God began to use various revivals in order to reveal to the church lost truths from His Word, truths that have existed from the day of Pentecost but that had mostly been abandoned by the fifth century. Throughout the Middle Ages, they were preserved only by small groups of believers here and there. There have been many revivals in history, and each one of these has reintroduced a truth, e.g., "justification by faith" brought by Luther. By looking at these revivals, we can see clearly that, every time, it has brought the church closer and closer to what the first church was that we read about in the Bible.

It did not stop with Martin Luther and the Reformation. Afterward came the Baptist revival, where God again revealed the "biblical baptism of believers" (full immersion based on one's personal faith). Later, the Methodist revival occurred, where the truth about "justification by faith" was revealed in a new way. Then there was the Adventist revival with "the hope of Jesus' second coming."

The next revivals renewed the focus on "baptism with the Holy Spirit" and the "gifts of the Spirit." The last big revival took place in Wales with Evan Roberts. This revival dealt with a renewal of the "five-fold ministry." The offices of apostle, prophet, evangelist, pastor, and teacher being given to the church by God received a new focus. To a large extent, they had become lost as a result of the Synod in 325 A.D., where they started to rebuild the church according to the structure of the Roman Empire, with the pope, bishops, priests, monks, and nuns, who later, through Protestantism, became replaced with pastors, bishops, and the board of elders.

As a consequence of all these revivals in which God has renewed truths from His Word, we have today various denominations, such as the Lutheran Church, Methodists, Adventists, the Pentecostal movement, and the Apostolic Church. All these revivals have been important, as they have brought a new understanding of lost truths. None of these revivals, however, dealt with the "structure" of the church. Again, the effect was the same as when you sow a new patch on old clothes.

Jesus is coming back very soon, and I am convinced that we are the ones who will see His return. Before His coming, He wants to prepare His church like a bride who is being prepared to meet her bridegroom. When we look at these revivals, it seems like the only thing we still lack is a reformation of the structure of the church. It has never been God's intention for these revealed truths to result in independent church denominations that, after a while, quench the fire of revival. God did not intend to create separate churches and denominations with their own "little" truth, while ignoring the other parts and, thus, hindering their members from gaining the whole truth.

Justification by faith is important, and it is the beginning of a new life in Christ, but after justification, there is a life to live in order to follow Jesus. In this life, we need to be baptized in water to bury our old sin nature and to rise to live in resurrection life in Christ. We also need justification by faith because Jesus did not die "just" to forgive us of our sins but also to break the power of sin, so that, in faith, we can live the holy life to which God has called us. In addition, we need the baptism of the Holy Spirit, among other things, in order to be able to live as disciples and followers of Jesus Christ and see the church grow.

Our starting point is not Martin Luther and the Reformation, nor is it one of the other revivals. Each of them only managed to present a small part of God's truth. Our starting point is the Word of God, the Bible, and Jesus Christ because, in Him, we have everything we need for life and godliness (2 Peter 1:3). This is also relevant when we look at the structure of the church.

I believe that we are coming close to the third reformation, but I also believe that this will be the last reformation before Jesus comes back. This is a reformation where God is going to put together all the pieces and prepare the church to meet her Bridegroom.

So, let the reformation begin.

—Torben Søndergaard

1

A THOUGHT EXPERIMENT

Some time ago, I wrote another book titled *Christian, Disciple, or Slave*. It is a journey back into the lifestyles of the first Christians. We took a particularly close look at what Jesus said in regard to following Him. In addition to that, we looked at the other names given to the first Christians, primarily "disciples" but also "Christ's slaves," as it actually appears many times in the original language. We discussed why it is important to dare to read the Bible as it is instead of constantly interpreting it according to what we see happening around us today.

The problem is that when we read in the Bible about following Jesus, we often look around us and think it is impossible and that it must be different today. It seems that, today, one does not need to sacrifice everything in order to follow Christ. This is at least what we often see and hear in our churches. We interpret the Bible according to our circumstances, experiences, and culture, which can be very dangerous. It can result in a situation where the blind are leading the blind. That is why it is so important that we let the Bible transform our understanding and not the other way around.

In my book, *Christian, Disciple, or Slave*, I presented a thought experiment, after which I asked a question: *If it was you, how do you think you would live? Do you think you would live like most Christians do today?*

In this book, *The Last Reformation*, I want to start with a similar thought experiment. I have changed the question somewhat, and I will ask some other questions afterward.

Try to imagine that there is not even one single Christian in the whole world. There are no churches, no Christian books, no Christian TV, or no Christian newspapers. There is nothing that directly has anything to do with Christianity, except for one Bible. One day, someone finds this Bible. He has never seen it before, nor has he heard about the Bible, Jesus, or Christianity, but soon he starts to read through the book.

He starts with the Old Testament about how it all began and how the land of Israel came into existence. He reads how God works with His people, and he gets a clear picture of God as holy and righteous. He reads about a God Who can get angry, but Who is also merciful and patient. A God Who has great love for His people. A God Who would one day send us all a Savior, which is the red thread throughout the Old Testament. When he gets to the end of the Old Testament, he already has an impression of what God is like and how He acts.

He continues by reading the New Testament where he sees the Savior that God had promised. He begins by reading the four Gospels that talk about how Jesus Christ went around preaching the gospel and healing the sick. Page after page, he reads how Jesus preached that people should repent and believe in the gospel, that everyone who wants to inherit the Kingdom of God should take up their cross and follow Him, and all the other radical things He said and did. The Gospels tell him how Jesus took His disciples and then sent them out to preach the gospel and heal the sick. He reads how Jesus was loved by some and hated by others. He reads how Jesus gave Himself on the cross for all of us and how, through His death and resurrection, He conquered death. Everything put together gives him a really good understanding of who Jesus was and what He preached.

He continues forward by reading Acts, where he sees that after Jesus' resurrection, He came and said that those who believed in Him would receive power from above when the Holy Spirit would come upon them. Then he reads about how it actually happened.

As he reads through Acts, he starts to understand how the first Christians lived. It was a life with a lot of opposition and persecution where it cost everything to follow Jesus. It was a supernatural life in fellowship with God and each other.

After Acts, he moves on to the Book of Romans. In the first four chapters, he reads that we have all sinned and gone far away from God. He goes to chapter five, which describes Jesus as the "new Adam" who forgives us and reconciles us with God. Chapters six through eight say that, in Christ, there is freedom from sin and that this freedom comes when one gets baptized and walks in obedience to the Spirit instead of the flesh.

After that, he comes to chapters nine and ten that explain how we can get saved by making Jesus our Lord. When he reads this, he bows his knees and asks Jesus to come and save him and to become his Lord. Then he immediately experiences the new birth the Bible talks about, salvation in Christ, and he soon gets baptized in the Holy Spirit, which one can read about over and over again in Acts. As he is sitting there on his knees, born again, he can feel a difference on the inside. He now knows that he has been forgiven and that what is written in the Bible is true because he has experienced it himself and has the inner witness. He gets up, determined to follow Jesus completely, and starts by baptizing himself because there is no one else to do it. From that moment on, he begins to live as a disciple based on what he reads in the Bible. He also sees others repenting and starting to follow Jesus. After some time, he and the other believers plant many churches around.

My question now is: *What do you think their churches would look like?* Would they look like the state church, or would they look more like our evangelical churches, or would they still look different from that maybe? Would their fellowship have a nice church building with a pulpit on a platform and all the chairs standing in neat rows? Or would they have no building, pulpit, or pews at all? Do you think they would have a service every Sunday morning, with a Sunday school on the side? Would they have a program consisting of a welcome, some songs, announcements and an offering, more songs, sermon, and then communion? Or would they have no program at all and simply allow the Spirit to guide them?

The truth is that their church would be very different from what the church looks like today. The problem nowadays is that a lot of what we do in church is not based on the Bible but on "Christian traditions," as well as paganism and national culture. I placed "Christian traditions" in quotes because many of the "Christian" traditions today actually come from Judaism and the Old Testament.

When we talk about culture, there is a need to distinguish between the different aspects of that culture, even though it can be difficult.

There is the aspect of culture within the church that I call "church culture." There are also national cultures that differ from country to country and from one ethnic group to another. We cannot now say for sure how they would form a church in the story I made up because it would certainly depend on the national culture they came from. If they, for example, came from a culture with strong family bonds, where they live together for many generations, it would influence their church in a different way than if they came from a culture that resembles the Danish one, where one does not always put so much emphasis on the family and family life.

The story does tell us one important thing about them, however. They would not have experienced any church culture and, therefore, would look for patterns in the Bible. This is contrary to our times, where a lot of what we do is based on traditions and church culture. That is why I know that their church would be much different from what we see in the Western world today. Much of what we do in the church today cannot be justified by examples from the Bible, but is based solely on church culture and traditions.

It is important that we try to distinguish between our national culture and the church culture. The national culture determines who we are as a people, regardless of whether one is a believer or not. Therefore, except for that which is unbiblical, there is no need to change the national culture. It, rather, is a strength to be able to relate effectively to unbelievers in our countries. The church culture, however, is a different story altogether.

Much of what the church is being built on today is based neither on the national culture nor on biblical teaching. Much of it is actually based on paganism and a church culture that goes back to the fourth century, a culture that already had changed from what Jesus represented and the way the first church lived for a few hundred years.

We do not need to impose our church culture on people in order to make them "proper Christians." Rather, when we remove today's church culture, we will see that people are more open to God. Most of them indicate they are willing to accept Jesus but reject the church as it is in many places. Let us, therefore, try to leave our church culture and the pagan traditions behind and see what the Bible has to say.

2

YOU WILL MAKE DISCIPLES

We will start by looking at the purpose of the church. When I look at churches in the West, I can see that they need to be refreshed.

I want to ask you some questions. *What is the purpose of the church? Is it having a large congregation?* Yes, of course, we want lots of people in the church, but did Jesus focus on gathering as many as possible, or did He emphasize something else? We see repeatedly that Jesus was never busy with the crowds. He did not leave a big church after three years of ministry here on earth, although He would surely have been able to get a huge church if He had wanted to. No, Jesus did not focus on the number of people. Jesus wanted people who were willing to follow Him and whom He could use to build His kingdom.

Is the purpose of the church to get a nice building and run a café, youth meetings, Sunday school, and so on? No, the first Christians did not have a church building, youth meetings, Sunday school, or much of what we associate with a good church today. Jesus did not talk about any of those things.

If the purpose of the church is not to gather a lot of people or get a nice building, then what is its purpose? The only purpose is what Jesus commanded us to do; namely, to go and make people into His disciples.

"All authority has been given to Me in heaven and on earth. Go

therefore and make disciples of all the nations, baptizing them in the name of the Father and of the Son and of the Holy Spirit, teaching them to observe all things that I have commanded you; and lo, I am with you always, even to the end of the age. Amen." (Matthew 28:18-20)

Jesus never said to His disciples that they should go out and build a lot of churches. No, He said they should go out and make disciples. He would build His church using them. This means that a nice big church building with many people is not necessarily a fulfillment of this purpose, unless all those people are made disciples and followers of Jesus Christ in everyday life. (My book, *Christian, Disciple, or Slave,* talks much more about this.)

The number of people, the buildings, or the finances should not be our focus when it comes to the question of whether a church is healthy or not. None of that matters if the church is not creating what Jesus has commanded, namely disciples. Jesus has not called us to start churches but to make disciples. A congregation or a church is not a purpose. No, it is God's means to His end of making disciples.

If we then have a church that has failed to fulfill this purpose, why do we continue in the same way year after year? Think of all the resources, money, time, and effort used to keep such a "machine" going, even though it still does not bring the results God wants.

Why do we keep inviting speakers from big churches, here and abroad, to come and preach when we have no idea how the people in their churches are living? Gathering people is not a big problem if you just give them what they want. Making disciples and followers of Jesus is something altogether different.

Not long ago, one of the bigger churches in Denmark organized a conference addressing "how to make disciples out of seekers." They were going to talk about the big challenge today of making disciples out of people in the church. But why does everyone look at that church and copy them when all they have accomplished is to make a bunch of seekers come to their church?

If Jesus came back today, would He take all seekers home with Him, or would He only take all the disciples? Many of the churches we perceive as big today are very small in God's eyes. When persecution starts for real and all things are revealed, everything will be turned upside down. The big churches will suddenly become small when they find out that following Jesus has a high price, a price most of them have never been willing to pay. This is precisely why they are going there and not to a place where the Word about repentance and self-denial is preached radically. It's very important that we focus on making disciples. We are living in a time when most of those in Christianity are gradually moving away from focusing on what the Word of God says. Today, many people look immediately at what seems to work right here and now. But we are not supposed to build something that can last only here and now. We have to build something that lasts forever!

We cannot judge the condition of a church by looking at the finances or the number of people, the church buildings, or the activities. The only way we can judge a church is by checking whether the people who go to that church are truly becoming disciples and followers of Jesus. Are they the ones who deny self, take up their cross, and follow Him? Do they obey the commandments that Jesus gave? Do they love God with their whole hearts and their neighbors as themselves?

To live as a disciple of Jesus is not an activity that you do for a couple of hours on a Sunday morning, while you're living for yourself the rest of the week. I think the way you live on a Friday night shows much more about your life with God than how you live on a Sunday morning. In the same way, what comes out of your mouth on a Saturday night better shows what is inside of you than what you say in church on a Sunday morning.

If we do not want to continue deceiving ourselves, we must dare to stop and take a real close look at the condition of our church, even if it shows a completely different picture than what we might be expecting. If you want to find out if your church is a healthy one, check how the young people live on Friday night, or look at what the church members talk about and what they entertain on Saturday night. That will give you a better idea of how you are going to end up if you continue on the same path as them. We become like those with whom we associate.

Instead of asking a church the question: "How many people do you have in your fellowship," we should rather be asking: "What do the young people from this church do on Friday night?" "What do the older members talk about when they are together with their friends from the church?" "How do you obey Jesus' commandment about spreading the Gospel?" The answers will definitely give a more accurate picture of how healthy that church is. The number of people, the buildings, the programs, the state of the finances, etc., are not the purpose in themselves. Instead, they can even be opposing the ultimate purpose of the church.

The purpose of the church is the fulfillment of the call that Jesus has given us to make people into His disciples by baptizing them and teaching them to obey everything He says. Let us therefore not become distracted by all these other things.

Some may ask, "Becoming a Christian is a journey that takes a long time for some people. Many of today's church members will become disciples after a while, don't you think?"

Let me say that this is how many people perceive it today, but we have to remember that people are not saved before they accept Christ as Savior and become born again. One is either a child of God or a child of the devil (1 John 3:10); born of flesh or born of the spirit (John 3:6); on the way to heaven or on the way to hell (Matthew 25:46). There is nothing in between. One can be a seeker and be "on the way," but if they are not yet born again, they will perish after death, no matter if they go to church, pray to God, or read the Bible. It means that all those who are only "on the way" in our churches will perish if they die before they get saved. If this was really understood, we would be preaching much more clearly and with consequence, which would cause many to repent right here and now.

If you study revival and church history, you will see that the acceptance of a long conversion that may take many years is a new phenomenon. We do not find it in the Bible. So preach the Word and expect that people will repent, and you will see it happen! If you preach another gospel that suits seekers, you will get seekers who never move on to repentance and salvation. Of course, there will be a handful who will repent after some time, but I can guarantee that we will lose even more who leave through the back door if we do it this way. In addition, we will not see the same radical conversions where people are willing to give everything to God.

Let us never accept any other purpose than the one Jesus has given us. He has not given us a commandment to go out and make seekers or church-goers. He said clearly that it is about making disciples—His followers—who obey what He has commanded us. When one grasps Jesus, one will also be willing to obey Him. He is the Life and the reason why we are here.

3

CHURCH CULTURE

What do you think of when you hear the word "church"? If you come from a Lutheran or Catholic background, you will certainly think of a church building with a big tower, an altar, and pews where people can sit when the priest is preaching. If you come from an evangelical background, you will surely think of a more modern building with a big stage and modern musical instruments. The pews are replaced with chairs that can be moved around, although they almost always stand in neat rows.

Even though what people associate with the word "church" can be slightly different, there are many things they have in common. The majority of people think of a building designed for the sake of worship. In this building, there is a stage or an altar, pews or chair rows, etc. These are some of the first things that come to mind. A church is a place where one goes to services, hears sermons, and does other church-related things.

What do you think of when you hear the word "service"? Again, the associations can vary from person to person. The common thing, however, is that people think of church as something that takes place in a building. There are songs, an offering, a sermon, and communion. The truth is that the things we think of do not necessarily come from the Bible; for example, a church building, stage/altar, pews/chair rows, etc. None of these things were known to the first Christians. They actually first appeared a few centuries after Jesus was here on earth and after the first church was started. The concept of a Sunday service that consists of songs, offerings, sermons, and communion cannot be found in the Bible either. The first Christians used none of these things that we consider necessary for us today to be a "proper" church or to be able to worship "properly." They had no special church buildings designed for services or other church traditions. Neither did they have an altar or stage where a special person could stand and preach the Word of God to a mass of people who sat and listened. Actually, they did not usually meet on Sunday mornings to have services, and they did not practice communion/the Lord's Supper the way we do today. All the things that seem to be so necessary today cannot be found in the Bible or in the description of the life of the first Christians. Maybe this is precisely why they experienced great progress. The truth is that the very things mentioned above can actually be a hindrance for progress and growth.

Today, when a pastor or priest on a Sunday morning with the Bible in his hand states: "Our churches are based on the Bible and nothing but the Bible," this is simply not true because a lot of what goes on in that church is not at all based on the Bible but on church culture and idol worship.

If we go back to the Christians we considered in the story at the beginning of this book, they did not have all these things we associate with a church today. They had not been impacted by church culture but only by what it says in the Bible.

The question, then, can be: "Does it matter what our meetings look like? We have to conduct our meetings in one way or another, so why can't we just continue doing it the way we have always done it?"

The answer is simple. If what you are doing is not directly unbiblical and does not hinder one from fulfilling Jesus' commandment to make disciples, it is, of course, all right to continue as you are doing. The unfortunate truth is, however, that much of what is done *is* unbiblical, and that is why it hinders us from making disciples as Jesus has commanded us to do.

As I mentioned before, people have different thoughts associated with the word "church," but one thing is certain: almost everyone thinks of a building, a place designed with the purpose of worshiping, etc. However, the concept of a special church building for that purpose is not found in the Bible. Further, it did not exist among the first Christians either.

We would have to fast-forward 300 years in church history before we could see the first "church" buildings as we know them culturally today. The first church buildings appeared during the reign of Constantine. Many of the things we do today find their roots around that time.

Constantine the Great was emperor of the Roman Empire from 306 to 337 A.D. He played a decisive role in the spreading of Christianity, but at a price. It happened at the cost of rejecting the Christianity that had been known for the first 300 years. Constantine transformed Christianity from a persecuted minority group into an authorized state religion. But Christianity cannot be forced upon people. One has to be born again from the heart out of free will, or else you will not be able to see the Kingdom of God. Forcing people to become Christians will never bring any good results.

Constantine introduced many changes, and one of them was the concept of church buildings. Until that time, Christians met together and broke bread in their homes. Church buildings have their source neither in the New nor the Old Testament but are the result of idol worship/paganism, which was a big part of Constantine's life. There was a period when he worshiped, among others, Sol Invictus, the god of the sun, and he wanted to include that worship in Christianity, thus making it a mixed religion. The holy day was shifted from Saturday to Sunday, which had originally been the day of the sun. He built temples on cemeteries and called them by the names of the dead so they could be worshiped. The churches faced the east so that the sun's rays (Sol Invictus) could fall on the faces of his self-appointed priests while they were conducting services. Look at these other practices that have their roots in paganism:

- *Why do we see Sunday as holy/as a holiday?* Because of the sun god.
- *Why do we have cemeteries outside many Lutheran and Catholic churches if we read in the Bible that the dead were buried outside the city gates?* Because of the old custom of worshiping the dead.

- *Why do Lutheran and Catholic churches traditionally face the east?* Because of the sun god.
- *Why are many Lutheran and Catholic churches named after a dead saint?* Because of paganism and worship of the dead.

The truth is that much of what we associate with Christianity today has its roots in the times of Emperor Constantine and others who lived in the centuries after the first Christians. This church culture is so deeply rooted in us that we often interpret the Bible in the wrong way because we have the wrong frame of reference.

If I say "service," then our own frame of reference interprets the meaning of the word. The same goes for the words "church" and "disciple," etc. It is my hope that this book can help the reader look beyond this church culture. If we can ignore it, we can start to understand what the Bible really says about how the church was meant to be and should be today. If we come back to what God intended, we will see Him adding daily to those who are getting saved.

4

OUR TRIP
TO THE GREEN FIELDS

Before we take a closer look at the different areas concerning church and service, I want to take you on a little trip. What I am presenting in this book is actually something that my wife and I were not able to see ourselves until some years ago, but God took us on a trip where our wrong understanding of the concept of church was removed. We no longer just go to church; we are the church. What God has done in us during the last few years is something we see Him doing more and more in the people around us today. We see that Jesus is about to build His church, a church that is not built of dead stones, programs, structure, memberships, church buildings, and so on, but a church built of living stones, led by His Holy Spirit, with Jesus Himself as the Cornerstone (Ephesians 2:20).

It has been a long trip for us, and we have learned a lot. It has been a lot harder to get rid of this wrong understanding than I thought it would be. Actually, until now, it has taken us almost twelve years, the planting of three churches, a lot of experiences, disappointments, opposition, mistakes, hours with the Bible and church history before we could say that we felt free to be the church God has created us to be.

In other words, it has taken me twelve years and the planting of three churches to come out of the church culture I had become a part of in the beginning. Today, I no longer go to an institution or a building we call "church." I am free from fear and other things that were planted in me due to control, which I will come back to later. I am the body of Christ here on earth, and I love the freedom this gives me. Life has become so much more exciting, and I want many more people to experience it. I can also see that the people who are around us today are growing much more than when we had "church" in the "old" sense. I am convinced that our circumstances and the structures that we are a part of have a huge influence on our personal growth.

As I share our journey with you, I hope it can help, encourage, and give you an understanding of how things connect together, seen from our evangelical perspective. I cannot go into too much detail without the risk of revealing too much about individuals. I will, however, pick out various important incidents that have influenced us and led us to where we are today. I also want to comment on what happened at that time and why it happened. It has been a long journey where we have repeatedly felt as if we were hitting a brick wall, until finally realizing we could move on.

Not long ago, I got the following prophetic word, which describes it really well. "I see that you, Torben, are standing with blood and blisters on your hands, while you are making a hole in a huge mountain. Lene is coming to help you, and the children are coming with water for both of you. On the other side of the mountain, there is a huge valley with green and fertile fields. I can see that you are making a way so that many others can go through the mountain and into those green and fertile fields."

I hope you want to go out to the green and fertile fields that are waiting on the other side of the mountain. It can be a long journey, depending on where you are, but it is worth it.

It did not take a very long time for Moses to get the Israelites out of Egypt where they had been in slavery (Exodus), but it took a great many years to "get Egypt out of them." It is the same today. It's not hard to come out of the church culture, but it is hard to get the church culture out of the individual. When it ends in success, it is like being born again. You suddenly see things in a totally new way and wonder why you could not see it before and why others cannot see it when you tell them how fantastic it is.

I was born again in April 1995. I come from a non-Christian family that did not have any special church traditions. If I had paid a visit to a Lutheran church, for example, I would not have had any idea when I was supposed to stand up or sit down during the service. Until the night I got saved, I had never set foot in an evangelical church either, and still it was not long before I started to adjust myself to the culture in which I found myself. The evangelical church where I got saved was a real faith fellowship in which much emphasis was put on "the man of God." They thought these "men of God" had a special connection with God, and one should therefore respect and honor them as if they were almost God Himself. I remember one particular experience some months after I got saved that really shows how fast one can become indoctrinated into a particular culture. It sounds like a joke today, but back then, it was also really terrifying.

I remember a day when I was in the church's bathroom washing my hands. Suddenly, I got a big shock because the door behind me opened and out came, yes, out of it came the "man of God" who was going to preach that evening. When I saw him, I thought: "What? Does he go to the bathroom just like everyone else?" Yes, that was the way I was thinking at that time. During that short period of time that I had been attending church, I had acquired a view of these men of God as being on a totally different level than us ordinary Christians. I can not say that others in the church thought the same way, but I was new in the faith and did not know so much about how the Kingdom of God functions. I thought these men of God were completely different and did not live the same way as us mortals. That experience still scares me today, and it shows how quickly one can start to think in a particular way, because of a certain church culture.

Since I first became a Christian, I have had a desire to serve God. It was not long before I became an usher in the church meetings. It was one of the few areas where I could serve God during the service in an evangelical church. I cannot sing, so the worship choir was not an option. I became the meeting's usher and was responsible for getting water for the big preachers, as well as standing by the door and welcoming people. I also quickly bought myself a suit because I had to fit in. I was really happy to be able to serve as a meeting's usher, but I also knew that I was called to do more. I was called to teach the Word of God to others, but I had no idea how I could reach that goal. One day, I asked my youth leader what I had to do to get to preach on the platform. His answer really impacted my whole future. He said the following: "Torben, you can become a Sunday school assistant. Then, after some years, you can become a teenage work assistant, and, again, after a few more years, you can become a youth leader. And as a youth leader, you will be allowed to preach one Sunday a year." I can still remember standing and counting with my fingers a total of five years. That meant that if I did all the right things according to that system, after five years I would be allowed to preach one Sunday a year.

That really made me think. I started to look at the others in the church who had been sitting there for many years but had not made much progress. This reality made Lene and me start talking about having to leave the church. If we had stayed, we would have become like the others who were sitting there year after year without making any progress. I would never have started to preach. It was not a bad church. It was actually good in many ways. But it suffered under the system that most of our churches are built upon today, a system where few people minister and a great number just sit passively and listen year after year.

During that time, we heard of a young married couple who were about to plant a church in another town. We paid them a visit and, as a result, left our church and moved to that other town.

When we moved there, we wrote the statutes for the church and started our first service. We were all very excited about how it would go, and I clearly remember standing together with the pastor and talking about how our first service should be. We were young and on fire for the Lord. We finally had an opportunity to do exactly what we wanted, and we did not want to just copy others. No, we wanted to let God do His work. But how could that be? We agreed that I would lead the meeting, and the pastor would preach. We were also going to take an offering, so we talked back and forth that we should not have the offering and the sermon right after each other. We agreed that I would welcome the people, and then we would sing some songs, take an offering, and have some more songs before he got up to preach. Yes, that was the plan, and we were both very excited about it, at least right up until I looked at the program and thought with disappointment: "This is not different at all! This is exactly how we held meetings in the other church."

I was really disappointed because I sincerely wanted to do something different. Today, it makes me think about the author Wolfgang Simson who said something like this: "The hardest part of starting a church that God wants is getting rid of our own understanding of what church is. This can take several years."

At that time, our understanding of service and of church was a hindrance to being able to do what God wanted. God has to remove the wrong concepts before He can continue to build with us. It's not always so easy, however, and those wrong concepts are a huge part of us and our church culture. I know many people who have started a church with a longing for something else and for making disciples, but after some time, they are left with a half-dead church where they entertain Sunday after Sunday without seeing any new disciples. Why? Because their church culture hinders them from doing what God wants them to do. They start sincerely, with big dreams, but they still end up with something they do not want at all—that which they ran away from, that which was the reason for them starting something new in the first place. For me, getting rid of the church culture has definitely been the hardest task.

When we moved to the new town, we also moved to a smaller fellowship. This suddenly gave me the opportunity to share from the Word of God. My turn to preach came. I remember sitting by the harbor, thinking about what I was going to say. I was browsing through the Bible and thinking about the sermons I had heard in the old church that were suitable for further use. I did not have much to give at that time. I still remember my first sermon. It was nothing special, but the most important thing was that I had started something, and I did not have to wait for it for five years. My turn came after just a few weeks, and Lene also found herself in the role of worship leader.

The reason we are where we are today is because we left the big church in the past. I know now that if we had not left then, we would never have reached our destination. It sounds tough, but I am convinced of the truth that lies behind it. When I look back, I can see that we are living a life today that is totally different from the life of many of our old friends. Many of them are actually not living with God any longer. I must sadly conclude that the system we came from has not managed to make disciples and minister as it should. Instead, it has slowly quenched people's zeal and fire for the Lord. This is true not only for our old church but for many churches in general.

It's sad to think that I had to leave the church to be able to make progress in my life with God. Look at how many are sitting in churches today merely listening and how few are really working and on fire for the Lord, even after so many years. Look around and think about how few ministries have been started by doing what the system has expected of them. The condition is similar in Lutheran churches, and there are many more denominations that lock people up within their system.

Recently, I received these prophetic words: "I can see a big pot with large flames. A lid is being put on the pot, and the fire is slowly being quenched and is dying out. I can see that God has given you a special call and grace to remove that lid so the fire can burst into flames again." This is what I really want to happen, even through this book.

It was difficult for us to be part of starting the church mentioned above since we were young and had no experience in leadership. It brought many challenges, and, after a year, we moved on. When I look back at our life, I can see that escaping from the other church was the beginning of an exciting walk with God. If I'm honest, I still do not know whether or not it was God's will that we move to that town and help the young couple plant the new church. I do know, however, that it gave us momentum so that God could later move us to where He wanted us. I wish many others would have the opportunity to do what we did, even though it was difficult. It is the best Bible school training one can get because we learn by doing and not just by hearing.

5

A NEW PLACE AND
ONE MORE CHURCH

Afte a year, we moved to another town in order to work
together with a friend. At the beginning, we went to an
evangelical church, but, after a short while, my friend came
to me and said that God wanted us to plant a new church. We knew
we were to work with him and agreed to start in our living room. He
was the pastor of the church, but we were both in the leadership, and
I worked as an evangelist.

We saw people getting saved and transformed, and the fellowship
was growing. As usual, the other churches in town were not particularly
excited about the new "rival." That is unfortunately how it is in the West
today, where we run churches like small companies that need to compete
for members and finances to keep running. This results in frequent
warnings against a new church to prevent "loss of the members." This is
an important reason as to why I have written this book.

We have to look beyond the ambition to build our own small
companies. If we are really free and working for the Kingdom of God,
then we would rejoice that the Kingdom is growing, instead of focusing
on the danger of losing members.

Our new church grew primarily with new people and not with
people from other churches. Even though the other churches did not
like us in the beginning, the cooperation improved after some time,
and we began meeting together with the other leaders from town. It

was in our very own living room that we seriously began to experience being used by God's Spirit.

I remember one evening when a lady suddenly fell on the floor, and a demon began to manifest itself through her. She was lying on her back, writhing sideways, and saying something in English with a very deep masculine voice. My first thought was: "Help, a demon! We have to find a pastor!" But then I realized: "Oh, no, there is no one here but me!" I had no choice but to pray and hope that God would help us. He did, and the demon left her. I began to see that what is written in the Bible really works. Since that time, we have cast demons out of many, and we have seen that God is the same today, just as we read in His Word.

Once again, I am convinced that I would never have acted if this had taken place in one of the bigger churches where it is the pastor, the board of elders, or a prayer team who do such things. This leaves a big flock that observes passively and never gets going. Fortunately, we had left the big church and now had to take this responsibility upon ourselves. After some time, we grew too large, and our living room became too crowded, so we rented a building where we could have our meetings.

I was happy that we were finally a "real" church with a venue, drum set, rows of chairs, etc. At first, we were all very excited, and we felt a little more "real" because we had another place to gather other than in our home. When we got the place together, however, with the rows of chairs, drum set, program, and everything else that a "real" church consists off, it felt as if we lost something personal that we had before. Many of the people slowly became passive viewers. After some time, we started to get frustrated and decided to divide the church into three groups to be able to go back to the good beginnings. The three couples in leadership got one group each, and we began to meet in our homes once again. This never really became successful, however, because we had separated the people from one another. Some people in our group would rather be in another, and vice versa. It never went back to what it used to be—an organic and living fellowship.

After some time of frustration in the church, we introduced some changes to how we ran it. As a result, I had to choose between the church and a mission organization, "Experience Jesus," that I had started. At the time, I was busy working in Experience Jesus and organizing meetings in various places. Now, however, we were going to build together in a new way, which meant that I would have to close down the organization.

There was a teaching that was very popular in some churches at that time. It went like this: "Let the seed die and obey your leader in everything, so you will succeed even more in due time." I could not do it. I could not close down Experience Jesus and stop traveling to meetings in various places, not even for a short time. We had to be faithful to the call God had given us. That is why we had no other choice but to stop our ministry in the church. Some other elders also resigned at that time. The period following was very hard for us, and we felt really down, but we received a word from the Lord: "Go, but take one step at a time." About a year after we left the church, it closed down, and the people started to go to other churches.

After we had decided to leave the church, a friend of ours called us and encouraged us to come to his Bible school. We agreed because we needed peace and some time to seek the Lord. Suddenly, the situation changed, however, and we found out we would have to close down our organization in order to go there. Again, it sounded as if we had to let the seed die before it could bring more fruit. I just could not do it, since I knew this work, this organization, was from God. I had to obey Him more than I obeyed people. As a result, we refused to go to the Bible school and did not know what to do next. It was a difficult time. As I said, the decision to leave the church had been ours, but it felt as though we had been thrown out of the fellowship that we had started, since we had no other choice but to go. Most of the people who went to the church had gotten saved through me, and they suddenly started to treat us like we were made out of thin air. We did not understand that either. Many years later, I found out they had been told by the leadership that we were experiencing a call to move on, and that was why we left. It made them think that it was us who did not want them anymore. That was one of the reasons nobody contacted us.

Some weeks after leaving the church, we were at a Bible camp. At the time, I felt we could not put up with the rejection any longer. One evening, I left the meeting and cried to God, ready to give up everything. The next evening, however, an African minister called me forward and gave me these words: "I can see you signing contracts. I can see documents being given to you. I can see you signing contracts, and you'll not pay yourself. I can see others paying. I don't care who did not stand together with you. I don't care who left you. There is someone who has been so meaningful in your life, but you should know that this separation is from God so that you don't become comfortable and miss your vision from God. If it went on, you would lose that vision, but God sent this separation and made you go through a desert so that you don't get dependent on anyone else other than God. Now your painful time is over, and you will see that God is going to pick you up from the dust and put you up on top of the mountain. Your pain is over. It's going to be a new day for you. It's going to be a new season for you."

It really was a great encouragement for us. It was true that the separation came from God. If we had stayed, we would have lost our vision. It really hit home. That was why I thought our wandering in the desert was over and from then on there would only be progress. The truth was that it was just the beginning. God was going to remove the wrong understanding of church from us, so He could build together with us. Little did we realize that the process was going to take the next five years …

6

WANDERING IN THE DESERT

We had no church, and we did not know what to do, but then a church from another town contacted us. They wanted us to come and help them. We met the leadership team, but I withdrew due to some particular issues including membership and submission to them. I could not agree to become a member of that church because, by doing so, I would also have to approve of everything that was happening there, which I could not. The church had a wrong view of re-marriage after divorce, and I could not accept that. Moreover, I was not able to find proof in the Bible for the idea of membership. In the previous church, we did not have to sign any papers in order to become a member. We were together, just like the first Christians.

Furthermore, the issue of having to submit to them was hard for me. Why should they make decisions for me concerning my life, as if I was still a child? At that time, I considered it very unhealthy, not because I did not want to do what the Bible said, but because leaders had tried to subdue/control me too many times in the past by saying that I should give up my vision or compromise on the Word of God. I was simply afraid it would happen again. I had to be faithful to God and His call instead of people's opinions. The issue of submission is a big problem in some evangelical churches. This does not mean that new believers are not to listen to their spiritual parents, but I think that mature Christians get locked up in a hierarchical system that stops them from making progress.

For this reason, we had some more talks, and the outcome was that we did not have to become members. I was supposed to preach one Sunday a month and could spend the rest of my time working for Experience Jesus. We considered this to be a good deal, so we decided to move to the town. With regard to the issue of submission, they said it would not be a problem, and it wasn't as long as I was within the system. However, they later used it against me in order to stop me from doing what I felt was God's will.

I am not writing about these things in order to let out hurt feelings but to give you an impression of how this system can work in some places. Through all of this, we have learned a lot, and, even today, we would not have wanted to miss any of it.

When we were supposed to move, we suddenly found ourselves with no place to move into. I remembered the words I had received about signing some papers without paying, so I thought it had to be about a house for us. I prayed and absolutely believed that God would give us a place to live. Fourteen days before we had to move, we still had no place to move into. Ten days before, we still had not found a place to live, so we felt pressured and sought God. Eight days before we had to move, a Christian man came by and said that God had told him to buy a house for us. All I had to do was find one. Seven days before the day we were to move, I found a beautiful house. I gave the papers to him. Later the same day, he called and said he had bought the house on the condition that the ones who had been living in the house for 33 years would move out within six days. They had agreed because they had a summer house into which they could move. The day we were supposed to move, we had a big house ready to move into. We were really happy and were praising God. The deal was that we would have to pay the house rent and all the house expenses to the man. As soon as we were able to take a loan from the bank ourselves, we would be able to become the homeowners, and the home equity would be ours.

We started to minister in the church as had been agreed upon, but within a short time, I was asked if I would like to be the youth leader because they had no one else for the task. We felt a little pressured but agreed. It went very well for a while, but after a time, I could see that it could not go on the way it was going. What we had experienced in our living room before had made a strong impression on us. As a result, our view of a Christian fellowship was much different from the view of the rest of the church. I could see that if we continued as the youth leaders, we would lead the youth group in one direction while the church went in another. Besides that, we could also see some theological differences. So we withdrew and started to seek God about what we should do.

Some time after that, I was on the Faroe Islands where God spoke to me through a prophetic word. When I came home, we knew it was time to take the next step, which was starting our own fellowship. We knew that the leadership would definitely not be happy about it, so I inquired with some other churches that were in the same network in order to find out what I should do. As a result, we gathered together, and I shared with them what kind of calling we were experiencing. We believed everything was fine then, but it was far from fine. Our understanding of things obviously differed, and the church leadership was not able to follow our view on fellowship. At the same time, they were really afraid of losing their members. As a result, others were warned against us, and we suddenly lost a lot of friends in the church. The man who owned the house changed his mind because of what happened. As a consequence, we missed the home equity worth forty to fifty thousand dollars, and we had to move again since he did not think the deal was valid any longer. It was really difficult, and we could not understand why there was so much trouble just because we were doing what we felt was our calling. Things did not work out, even though we really tried to do it by the book.

Why are the churches so afraid of new fellowships if all the numbers show that this is the solution to reaching the world? I felt particularly hurt because of the issue with the house. I had experienced before that people called me names and told lies about me, but this time, it also affected my wife and children. They had been so happy to live in the house, and we had some nice neighbors with whom our children could play. I tried to talk to the other churches in the network, but it seemed they did not care what we thought. It was just us against a bigger church, so nothing more happened.

The story of suddenly being warned in advance is unfortunately not a singular event. Later on, I met an African who had left the same church in the same town some years before and started an international fellowship. He experienced exactly the same problem, having suddenly been accused of "heresies" and being warned against, which resulted in his losing a lot of friends. In many ways, our "system" resembles that of Jehovah's Witnesses. This might be hard to understand before being in a similar situation oneself. Since then, I have met so many people who have left the "system" and have told me about their experiences afterward that I can say it is not totally wrong to say that it reminds me of the Jehovah's Witnesses' practice of ostracism.

7

VISITED BY ANGELS

During that time of upheaval, we also received some great encouragement. We were visited by some very special people who became a great blessing in our lives. In an unusual way, I got in contact with a married couple from Canada who live in the Netherlands six months of the year. Their names are Steve and Marilyn Hill. I talked to Steve about our situation over the phone, and even though we had never met before and they did not know us at all, they jumped into their car and drove all the way from the Netherlands to Denmark to pay us a visit. It was such a blessing because, for the first time, we got to meet someone connected to a house church network who really understood us. Having them over for a visit was great. I came to understand that our view of what church should be like was absolutely biblical and that we were not alone in this. So many times before, I had experienced the feeling that I did not fit into the church system and that something must be wrong with me. Their visit opened our eyes and showed us that we were not crazy.

When they left after a few days, Lene said: "Have we just been visited by angels or what?" It was so great and felt so unreal to us that such mature and experienced people had been willing to travel such a long way to meet us. Out of this first meeting developed a good friendship and a connection to a network that we are still cooperating with today. Steve Hill was like a father to us, one who only wanted us to succeed and who had no ambition in any way to use us to build his own vision. For the first time, I felt I had met a leader I could submit to with all of my heart.

Since we had to move out of our house, we bought an older house, and I started to renovate it. At that same time, we started a new church, or whatever we should call it. The church consisted of two newly saved young people and our family. In some ways, it felt like taking a step backward. After all, we were used to gathering with about 20 people in the youth group. But, today, I know that it's better to build from scratch and do it properly.

During that time, I made a big mistake for which I later had to repent. When we got started, there was a lot of gossiping going on about us. People were saying that I had caused problems, that I had been rebellious, and that I did not want to submit. Sadly enough, gossip flourishes in our churches nowadays. Nobody, however, came to us and listened to our side of the story. Because of all the criticism, I wanted to prove that I was not on the wrong track and that I had started a church. I therefore sent a press release to a Christian magazine called "Udfordringen" ("The Challenge") and created a website for our church so that people could see we were a "real" church. I did so despite the fact that I clearly experienced God telling me not to enter into such a system again but that we should just meet at home, without a website or an organization, etc. Unfortunately, I did not listen. I felt such pressure and wanted so much for the criticism to end that I did not listen to what God wanted but went along with the idea anyway. By the way, this does not mean that it is wrong for a church to have a website, but the motive behind it is important.

Starting this new fellowship and officially announcing it as a church also meant that I had suddenly become a pastor. With the other church plantings we had been involved in, there had always been somebody else, but now it was just me. With this, something unpleasant happened on the inside of me. Suddenly, a big pressure fell upon me that even felt demonic. With the responsibility also came all kinds of questions. One of them in particular weighed upon me heavily, and that was the number of people we had in the church. This question was really embarrassing for me because we were only five or six people, and I now felt as if everything depended on me. If everything went well with the church and the people, it meant that I was a good pastor, but if not, it too seemed to be my fault. This caused me to lose the focus I had before when I simply worked for the Kingdom of God without being responsible for a particular church. When someone got saved in another town through my ministry or my website, I just directed them to a local church and was glad the Kingdom of God was growing. Now, I felt I was to be held accountable for the wellbeing of this church, the people in it, and how many there were. It even felt like a competition to me where it was all about which church gets the biggest numbers and which church has the best people. The other churches had now become rivals with whom I had to compete.

I remember a particular day when someone from another part of Denmark got saved through the website. I tried to convince him to move to our town so that our numbers would grow. Doing so felt terrible, and I remember asking God to help me because I could not understand what was going on with me. I also got an unhealthy drive to see the members of my church succeed. Because of this, I started to control them even though I really loved them and truly wanted the best for them.

Fortunately, I was set free from all this later. I can, however, imagine that all of this might sound quite extreme to you if you do not know what it is like to be a pastor in the church culture we have created. This is the reason why so many pastors of churches resign or burn out. It is because of stress. It is also why so many church members feel abandoned or imprisoned by control when they want to move on. Experiencing these things myself really gave me a new understanding of these dynamics. Luckily, not all pastors think that way, but the truth is that the body of Christ has been divided into small "companies" that often cannot work together, especially when they are from the same town and have to compete for the same potential "customers."

What happened next was that Lene became sick due to fear and stress. Among other things, it was caused by the things we went through—opposition, moving, loss of friends, etc. At the same time, we were pressured financially. We had lost a lot of money, and I had also suddenly lost my job because I had been telling my colleagues about Jesus. We ended up in a difficult situation without any regular income, and we had a big old house that badly needed renovation.

When all of this happened, I really felt I did not want to live anymore. The opposition we had experienced in the last years and our current situation gave us a lot of pressure in many ways. I was tired of it all and did not know what to do. We had truly ended up in a desert, and it seemed it was not to stop any time soon. We were seeking God intensely, and, during one period of time, I actually prayed between eight and ten hours every day because I could not do anything else. Things slowly started to change, and one night God gave me a dream that made a huge impact. In that dream, I saw myself standing with two men who were smoking. One of them reached out his hand with a cigarette and said I should smoke it. I refused, but he insisted and said I had to smoke it or else people would notice that they were smoking. I took the cigarette and started to smoke it, even though I knew I should not. Then I woke up.

I knew that the dream was from God, and I immediately understood its meaning. The other two men represented the churches we had helped to start. I represented the church we had at that moment. The cigarette and the smoke represented the whole system that contaminates the body and kills life. God did not want us to become part of that, but because of the pressure and fear of what others would think, I had smoked the cigarette, so to speak. I felt so bad when I realized what I had done. I was tired of myself and knew very well where I had been "smoking." It had to do with the fact that I had sent the press release to the Christian newspaper and made our website for the church. I had been feeling such pressure, due to the fact that others considered me to be rebellious and did not think our church was a "real" one. That was why I did it, even though God only wanted me to trust Him. As a result of this, I suddenly had become part of the church system again.

That same day, my friend Steve Hill called me and said that he would be coming over to visit us. He really appeared at the right moment. When he arrived, we talked about the dream, and he could easily see how I had started to resemble the system we had left. The first time Steve had been to our place, I had been walking back and forth in our living room struggling with a wrong understanding of the church. Even though I was able to follow his line of thinking and saw in the Bible that what he said was right, the other view of the church was still deeply engrained in me! This time, I was again walking back and forth, saying to myself: "When will you learn that, Torben? When will you learn that?" Yes, it's really hard to get out of that system and trust God alone.

After this, I gathered the church together and told them about my dream and asked for forgiveness. I closed down "the church" and the website. The people were there all the time, and we kept on meeting, so all that we actually closed down was the "system." But it was important for me to close it down and start all over again. A lot happened afterward. A fresh wind came and "took over" the church, and we saw many new churches starting around us. God had finally led us through the desert and called us back to our old town where we are living again today.

Those five years in the desert were really difficult but also necessary. They were necessary to get rid of the church system in us and to teach us to depend only on God. Now I finally feel free from that system and from what people expect of me.

The recent times have been very powerful for us. We have seen God moving more powerfully than ever before, and many lives have been transformed. We know that this is something God wants to do all around today. We are going to see people coming out of church systems and into the green, fertile fields. We are going to see Jesus building His church—a church that is not based on membership, control, and outward structures, but a church guided by His spirit and built of living stones, that is, His disciples. A church that is happy to see people move out and start their own families in the neighborhood instead of waging war with them. What kind of parents would be happy if their children were still living at home at the age of 40? Or, who wants to live with Mom and Dad throughout their whole life? The same goes for a biblical church, which is supposed to be like a family.

I am convinced that God has taken us through all of this so that we could learn how to trust Him and how to be free from the system. Although it has been really difficult, we do not bear a grudge against anyone. Yes, the brothers "threw us into the well," just like in the story of Joseph, but God was with us and brought us here so that we could set His people free today. He has been with us in every situation and used it for His purpose. I know that God uses whom He wants for whatever purpose He wants, and this is why I can forgive anyone. Sometimes we do not understand it, but later we see God's presence in everything that happened. Therefore, I want to encourage you to go the way you're supposed to go even though it can be hard because there is freedom and victory on the other side of the mountain. Today, we do not just go to church, we are the church. Ever since I got saved in 1995, I have heard that the body of Christ does not consist of buildings but of us Christians. Only now do I understand what it really means. We can see that God is really building His church, a church that is not built of stones, programs, finances, fear, and control.

I hope that our journey will encourage you and give you an understanding of many of the things that happen in churches today. I'm sure that many will recognize a lot in what I have been describing.

8

FINANCES

When I look at churches today, I can see that church buildings are the biggest challenge. Having a church building is not necessarily wrong, but it often implies many other things that can sabotage God's ultimate purpose with the church.

Let's take a look at finances. A lot of money is needed to pay for buildings, chairs, carpets, heating, and all the other necessary things. Because of this, the church members quickly become essential for maintaining the church. With an increase in members, the expenses rise as well. Because of this, having many church-goers does not necessarily mean that one has a huge surplus in the budget. On top of this, the pastor with responsibility for the church is being paid a salary by the church. This means that members are not only essential for maintaining the church but also for the pastor's personal income.

Imagine a church with 80 members and a yearly budget of about $300,000. From this money, about $60,000 is paid out as the pastor's salary, and ten to fifteen percent goes to missions, which, according to research, is the norm in churches today. This means that the rest, which is more or less $200,000, is used to keep the church running. The biggest expenses are usually the mortgage on the church building, furniture and maintenance. Due to the fact that these expenses often increase with a growth in church membership, this situation is not likely to easily change. Let us then imagine that a married couple from the church experience a call to move on. Or, even "worse," they feel called to start a fellowship in their own home. This means that two tithe payers leave the church. Let's say that these two members have been paying about $10,000 in tithes to the church every year, and now this income suddenly disappears. Imagine how that $10,000 will impact the budget of such a church, especially if the church already has a tight budget. Now, imagine what happens if one or two more couples experience a call to go away and become missionaries. The truth is that many churches today are run as businesses. Church-goers become paying customers that are needed to keep the church running.

Imagine that a mature married couple who have been living with God for many years come to the pastor and say: "We've really been seeking God, and we feel that it's time for us to move on. We would like to have your blessing." Do you think the pastor will bless them? I feel that if there was no money issue involved, and if the pastor had nothing to lose, he would bless them with great pleasure. It should be every parent's wish that the children will one day leave home and start their own family. It's a good thing to be ready to move on and stand on your own two feet. Even Jesus lived with His disciples for only a short time before He sent them out. It's a leader's job to make people dependent on God and not on themselves, to lay a foundation in their life that they can later build on themselves. If we talk about what is natural, we can easily all agree that it's unnatural for a 40-year-old to still live at home with his or her parents. The same rule applies to the Kingdom of God, and this is exactly the way Jesus and the first Christians discipled people.

The truth is that where finances are tight, there is often much control to keep people in the church. And this is the reason why some pastors would answer the parishioners above: "No, I don't think you're ready, and you have to obey your leader." Unfortunately, we are not talking here about rare incidents. I have experienced it many times, and I consider the concept of "church as a business" to be the main reason for it. Unfortunately, pastors who are dependent on the church members' money to keep the church running too often let themselves be controlled by finances rather than by what the Word of God says. Instead of releasing people into their ministries, they instead want to use them to fulfill their own visions.

I am not out to criticize pastors but to see them as victims of this system. I feel sorry for them, and I want to save them from it. The problem is not them, or any other people! No, it's the whole church system we have built up.

The need for finances even affects situations where there is sin in the camp. The Word of God outlines the proper procedures for addressing sin in the church. It involves admonishing the sinner and, as a last resort if they remain unrepentant, excluding the sinner(s) as the Bible says. In the current church system, it is also about finances. In this current system, when a sinner is expelled from the church, one does not just say goodbye to a person who is choosing to rebel against God and live in sin but also to a stack of money. This, unfortunately, results in many churches compromising the Word of God when it comes to preaching about what sin is and how we should react to it. Just a few months ago, I had a talk with a pastor about some of his church members he did not feel comfortable about and who had caused a lot of destruction in the church. I asked him why he did not let them go, to which the pastor replied: "We need their money." Money is the reason why so many do things they should not do and fail to do things they ought to do. This is often a cause of great stress for pastors.

Some time ago, I heard this powerful quotation: "Christianity started out in Israel as a fellowship; it moved to Greece and became a philosophy; it moved to Italy and became an institution; it moved to Europe and became a culture; it came to America and became an enterprise."

Unfortunately, we can no longer say that it is only like that in America. To a large extent, the same thing is true about Denmark and the rest of Europe.

An enterprise is the same as a business. The church is the body of Christ. If a body is transformed into a business, is that not prostitution? That is why we do not find any church buildings or employed pastors in the first fellowships. They did everything in a very different way compared to today, and that includes finances.

If we look at the Danish Lutheran Church, it becomes even worse. The state, or "people's," church runs about 2,300 churches and employs about 2,400 pastors. The church tax is not enough to keep the system running, so on top of the church tax, the state donates 180 million dollars every year. The turnover of the state church becomes thus one- to two-billion dollars. This means that the state has influence on the church. It is no longer God's church but the state's, just like it is called. In addition, we see more and more how the church adapts in putting the state and the people above the authority of the Bible.

My own opinion is that we should close down the state/Lutheran church completely, since it corrupts people and creates a church culture that is not biblical. If you ask a non-Christian in Denmark what he thinks of when he hears the word "Christianity," the most common answer you will receive reflects on the Lutheran church: it is buildings and doctrine. When you look on a world map, you will see that the Lutheran church is rather small. When including the Catholic church, there are around 2 billion Christians in the world. The Lutheran church has just over 70 million members, a rather small percentage. The Pentecostal and Charismatic movements contain around 800 million people. All in all, that is over 10 times more than the Lutheran church. However, it is the Lutheran church that overshadows everything in Denmark and influences the picture most Danish people have of Christianity. The state church culture is so deeply imbedded in most of us that it even influences the culture of the free churches. As you will see later in this book, there is a huge difference in the state church and how Christianity functioned two thousand years ago. I say, close down the whole system and put the money into something else!!

9

TITHING

Let's look at the idea of church as business. Most free churches nowadays follow the principle of paying tithes. For those who are not familiar with the concept, it means that believers should be paying ten percent of their income to the church they are attending.

The state church in Denmark is not familiar with the principle of tithing but is financed through the church tax. If you were to take away the baptism of babies you would end up taking away most of their members, too, which, in turn, would take away their economy. In that way, the state church would soon die out. The state church is controlled almost entirely by money. The baptism of babies is an important part of the church because it brings in money. There is a big fuss about baptizing babies that does not actually have biblical support. The idea of "baby baptism," as I call it, comes from the 4th Century. Investigation into the history of baby baptism shows that it was almost always linked to church membership and therefore had an economical side, too.

Let's look again at the free churches. What would happen if we took away the tithing principle from the free churches? It would mean that many free churches would have to close because they are built entirely around this principle.

You might be thinking that tithing actually belongs to the church and is a biblical principle. The truth is, however, that tithing is not a New Testament principle the way we teach it today, which means that many are building churches on a wrong foundation.

Many Christians in the free church have heard these words from the book of Malachi:

"Will a man rob God? Yet you have robbed Me! But you say, 'In what way have we robbed You?' In tithes and offerings. You are cursed with a curse, for you have robbed Me, even this whole nation. Bring all the tithes into the storehouse, that there may be food in My house, And try Me now in this," says the Lord of hosts, "If I will not open for you the windows of heaven and pour out for you such blessing that there will not be room enough to receive it." (Malachi 3:8-10)

"You are stealing from God if you don't pay your tithe," the pastor will say. "It belongs to the church. The tithe belongs to God and should be paid to the storehouse, which is the church to which you belong." In some free churches, this is as well known as John 3:16. The truth is that many pastors who are using this argument might be stealing from God themselves. They first misuse the Bible and then the money, spending it on something other than what God has said.

Do you know what the text in Malachi is referring to when it mentions tithes and offerings? Do you know what the offering is truly for? Do you know that there are different forms of tithes? Of course, not. Most do not consider this because the only thing they have ever heard is that tithing means giving ten percent of their income to the church. I dare to say that most Christians who pay ten percent of their income to the church do not know to what Malachi is referring.

Did you know that when you were going to pay your tithe, sometimes you needed to pay an extra fifth?

"If a man wants at all to redeem any of his tithes, he shall add one-fifth to it. And concerning the tithe of the herd or the flock, of whatever passes under the rod, the tenth one shall be holy to the Lord." (Lev. 27:31-32)

Did you know the Bible says you yourself were sometimes to eat of your own tithe?

"You shall truly tithe all the increase of your grain that the field produces year by year. And you shall eat before the Lord your God, in the place where He chooses to make His name abide, the tithe of your grain and your new wine and your oil, of the firstborn of your herds and your flocks, that you may learn to fear the Lord your God always." (Deut. 14:22-23)

Did you know that tithing in Israel was from the land and not of money?

But if the journey is too long for you, so that you are not able to carry the tithe, or if the place where the Lord your God chooses to put His name is too far from you, when the Lord your God has blessed you, then you shall exchange it for money, take the money in your hand, and go to the place which the Lord your God chooses. And you shall spend that money for whatever your heart desires: for oxen or sheep, for wine or similar drink, for whatever your heart desires; you shall eat there before the Lord your God, and you shall rejoice, you and your household. You shall not forsake the Levite who is within your gates, for he has no part nor inheritance with you. (Deut. 14:24-27)

That's right. It says here, too, that you were to eat it yourself. Did you know that, every third year, your tithe was to stay at home? It was to be fed to the fatherless and the widows.

"At the end of every third year you shall bring out the tithe of your produce of that year and store it up within your gates. And the Levite, because he has no portion nor inheritance with you, and the stranger and the fatherless and the widow who are within your gates, may come and eat and be satisfied, that the Lord your God may bless you in all the work of your hand which you do." (Deut. 14:28-29)

As you can see, we have taken from the Bible without knowing what it really means and have built up a whole church system on it. We could continue to see more examples in Scripture indicating that the way the church teaches about tithing is just one of the tithes we see in the Bible. The fact is that there are many different types of tithes. There was, for example, a tithe to the Levites because they did not get any land as an inheritance, and, in turn, they were to pay a tithe out of their own to Aaron and the other priests (Numbers 18).

There was also a celebration tithe that was to be transported to Jerusalem and was used for celebrations. Then, as we read earlier, there was the tithe for the poor that was to be paid every third year.

It is also worth noting that Abraham did not pay a tithe with his own money but from the spoils of war, and this happened only once during his entire life, according to what we read. All these examples show that the issue of tithing is not as simple as it seems. One thing becomes clear, however, and that is the fact that the "storehouse" is not necessarily the local church.

The reason I stated that pastors are actually sometimes the ones stealing the tithes is that the tithe was not meant to finance a church building and all that is included. The primary goal was to support those who worked in the temple, because they had not any land of their own, and the widows and the poor, so that they could eat and be full.

Nowadays, the tithe goes to large buildings and paychecks for pastors who are doing the lot of things that the people should be doing themselves. Today, we are all God's priests. The service of the Levites in the Old Testament is over, and we should not try to maintain it. We often even forget about the widows and the poor who are among us. Why not pay the tithes to them and get a little more biblical?

The early church did not spend money on big buildings or pastor's paychecks. The money was used according to the needs in the fellowship and was given to those who were traveling and had the task of spreading the gospel and equipping the saints. The Bible does not require us in any way to pay ten percent of our income to the local church with which we are affiliated.

Okay, then, but did Jesus not say that we should pay a tenth of our income?

> *"But woe to you Pharisees! For you tithe mint and rue and all manner of herbs, and pass by justice and the love of God. These you ought to have done, without leaving the others undone." (Luke 11:42)*

No, Jesus did not say that we should give a tithe. He said that the Pharisees should pay a tithe. The reason for that was that they were a part of Israel, and tithing and tributes were part of the tax system that God had ordained at that time. They were to give a tithe of crops and of cattle. In connection to what Malachi writes to them, they rob God if they do not pay this tax because it was there to support the land of Israel.

The truth is that only a few people know what tithing is really all about. So when someone today says that you should pay ten percent of your income to the church, which is the storehouse, well, that person either does not know the written Word or is misusing it consciously to finance their work.

I am not saying that it is wrong to pay ten percent of your income. I actually mean to say that ten percent is a good start. But the way I see it, according to the New Testament, all our money belongs to God and not just ten percent. Tithing can be a really good thing, and I think that we should give with a joyful heart if we are to give. But tithing can actually keep people in their comfort zones. They can easily begin to think that since they have given their ten percent, the rest is theirs. But, no, my friend, everything you have belongs to Him, and you shall one day be held accountable for how you used it (Matthew 25). The Bible has a lot to say about giving. If you have become confused by all of this, go and search the Scriptures yourself and ask God what you should do with your money.

Why did I bring up such a delicate subject? I know all too well that this is a fuse waiting to be lit and can cause a lot of problems. The reason I bring it up is to show you that a lot of churches are built on a false foundation. A foundation that helps to hold up a system that is simply not functioning properly. This system traps people and prevents them from obeying God. It is a system that stresses out the pastors and obstructs us from spreading the gospel and training disciples. Many church-goers wish they could spend their money to support other causes, but they simply will not do it because of what they have been taught. Instead of giving to the poor, widows, and the spreading of the gospel, which is what the Bible tells us to do, they are giving their money to buildings, chairs, sound equipment, etc, and mostly out of fear. Think about the hundreds of thousands of dollars that could be spent in other ways to reach out with the gospel to the world.

The money would truly start be used for what God really wants to achieve. Imagine a fellowship in which a married couple decides that, this month, they will give their tithe, or a suitable sum, to a single mother of three within the fellowship. Wow, it would spread like wildfire as soon as people heard. "In their fellowship they actually help each other." Imagine all the young people who could be sent out to spread the gospel.

The teaching that says ten percent of your income should go to the church certainly does keep the church going, but it takes the focus away from what God has planned and from what we read in the New Testament.

"Now all who believed were together, and had all things in common, and sold their possessions and goods, and divided them among all, as anyone had need." (Acts 2:44-45)

Even so the Lord has commanded that those who preach the gospel should live from the gospel. (1 Cor. 9:14)

As you can see, economy plays a big role in today's churches. It traps people and creates passivity. When you pay a pastor to hear from God for you, which you are called to do yourself, you are inevitably going to become passive. The pastor quickly becomes the professional middleman between God and man.

If you are now thinking, "Yippee, I don't need to pay my tithe anymore and can spent it all on myself now," I would like to tell you that, in doing so, you would be revealing that God is not Lord over your money. If you belong to Him, then so does your money. This teaching should, instead, make you search the Lord to be free to give even more but to give to those you feel led to give it to. God will surely bless it!

"But shouldn't I obey the church that I'm a part of and give my tithe there?" If you are a member in a church where one is expected to give tithes, then you can, of course, continue to do so, as long as you are a member or until the discipline changes. The fact that some churches decide to impose on people to give ten percent of their income in order to be a member is something I do not wish to comment on. It is not biblical, but it is not a sin either. It is up to each individual church to decide whether to enforce tithing or not. The individual church will give an account before God as to what the money was used for. It should not be taught, however, that it as a biblical law because it is not. People should be free to decide whether they want to be part of the church or not. If some stop paying their tithe and therefore stop being a member, it does not mean that they are disobeying the Bible. It is not the Bible that says one must give ten percent.

It is not a problem for me that some churches choose to take in ten percent of their member's income. The problem comes in when churches consider it stealing when people decide not to tithe to the church, or that they are considered to be disobedient to God and under a curse if they continue, or if they decide to stop being a part of the church. Both are examples of stealing—stealing people's money and stealing their freedom to serve God.

"But what about all the testimonies of people who have been blessed by giving tithes?"

There are indeed a lot of testimonies about people who have been blessed by giving ten percent of their income, but I believe they were blessed for giving, not for giving exactly ten percent of their income to a specific church. If you give in faith, God will bless you. It says so in His word. If you experience that God is saying ten percent, and you are obedient, He is going to bless your obedience. If He says to give fifteen percent, or a certain amount, and you give it, it is the same. If He says you should give to some missionaries or others in the fellowship, then He will surely bless it. God loves a joyful giver, and He blesses those who give in faith.

I have many testimonies from people who have stopped giving ten percent to a church and, instead, gave a different sum to a number of others and suddenly experienced blessings. It is not the ten percent that counts. It is the obedience, just as God says. And, yes, giving ten percent to a fellowship could be part of this.

10

A Tool For Missions

Before we move on and take a look at how the church functioned in the beginning, there is something we first need to come to grips with. In order to do so, I am going to ask you a question: *Do you see the church as a place where Christians come together to become equipped, or is it a place where non-Christians should come to hear the gospel?*

Your answer to this question is vital. If the purpose of the church is to equip Christians, then the entire focus will be on how to do this the best way possible. However, if the purpose of the church is to be a place where non-Christians can become Christians, then the focus will be on something completely different. The focus will be on finding the best way to bring non-Christians to church and how to keep them there. Therefore, it's very important to have a clear idea of what the purpose of the church should be.

The idea of the church being a place where non-Christians can come and hear the gospel is actually a relatively new idea. We do not have to go back many decades to find a completely different idea about the purpose of church. In those days, the church was a place where Christians could come together to be edified and to be discipled.

When pastors and leaders talk about the church today, they are mostly focused on how to get non-Christians to come to their church. Instead, they should be looking to God to find the best way to equip the Christians who are already there. This would actually give an entirely different and more biblical focus for the purpose of the church.

The first fellowships were simply Christians coming together. When they were together they were one in spirit and in truth. They were one, and they had all been born again into the same family. They all had the same longing—Jesus Christ. For that reason, and that reason alone, they could share their lives in fellowship and grow together in the Lord. Whenever they came together, they also shared communion, which was not just a little bit of bread and wine. No, it was part of a meal they ate together. Regardless of whether you share communion the way we read about it in the Bible or you do it like the majority of the Christians do today, communion is still very powerful. It's not something to be taken lightly.

These verses are often read with regard to communion:

> For I received from the Lord that which I also delivered to you: that the Lord Jesus on the same night in which He was betrayed took bread; and when He had given thanks, He broke it and said, "Take, eat; this is My body which is broken for you; do this in remembrance of Me." In the same manner He also took the cup after supper, saying, "This cup is the new covenant in My blood. Do this, as often as you drink it, in remembrance of Me." For as often as you eat this bread and drink this cup, you proclaim the Lord's death till He comes. (1 Cor. 11:23-26)

But this can be a catastrophe if we simply leave it here as many do today. We need to read the following verses, too:

> Therefore whoever eats this bread or drinks this cup of the Lord in an unworthy manner will be guilty of the body and blood of the Lord. But let a man examine himself, and so let him eat of the bread and drink of the cup. For he who eats and drinks in an unworthy manner eats and drinks judgment to himself, not discerning the Lord's body. For this reason many are weak and sick among you, and many sleep. For if we would judge ourselves, we would not be judged. But when we are judged, we are chastened by the Lord, that we may not be condemned with the world. (1 Cor. 11:27-32)

Communion is something much more than "just" a meal with food or a little bread and juice. This meal has a spiritual effect that is very powerful and that might even be negative if it is being dealt with in the wrong way. Therefore, it is important that we do not let just anybody take part in communion like we do today. We read here that it can result in the person eating and drinking judgment on themselves. The church needs to be a place for those who have Jesus as their Lord and are living with Him.

I recently read of a pastor who said he no longer had a problem with non-Christians taking communion. He said this because he had read that Judas had taken communion, and he did not have the right relationship with God. He said this in order to defend the fact that, in his church, those who were not born again were allowed to take part in communion. But Judas is a very bad example to use in this case because we read how Satan came into him and that, after some time, he betrayed Jesus and then died.

Communion has always been set apart for Christians, and it should be like that even today. The lack of understanding that the church, and communion, are meant for Christians might have very negative consequences.

The popular idea of the church being a place where non-Christians can come and meet God is a new way of thinking. Why not invite people into your home to have dinner instead and meet them where they are. Then you can share the gospel with them yourself and even baptize them in your bathtub! That way, they already have a natural relationship with those who led them to Christ instead of the unnatural relationship they often have to a pastor who does not really know them. It is obviously the best and most biblical way to do it. Afterward, you could take this new Christian with you to the gatherings of the church you join. Then, when they are there, they will not be amazed as to why people, for example, speak in tongues. It is no longer strange to them because they do it as well! This is actually the way things are done in a lot of other countries, especially in those countries where Christians are being persecuted, and where the church is growing a lot more than it is here in the West.

Unfortunately, many have taken away speaking in tongues and

other controversial things from the church in order to accommodate non-Christian seekers. That is not only unbiblical, it's also dangerous.

Someone asked me whether we pray in tongues when we meet, and I answered yes. She then told me that it was not biblical since Paul says:

> Therefore if the whole church comes together in one place, and all speak with tongues, and there come in those who are uninformed or unbelievers, will they not say that you are out of your mind? (1 Cor. 14:23)

My answer to that is: "We do not have uninformed or unbelieving people coming to our meetings! However, if an unbeliever happened to join us, we would naturally take that into consideration. We would take the opportunity to teach them about the Holy Spirit and speaking in tongues, and that would mean they would no longer be uninformed! Instead, our speaking in tongues would become a sign to them, one that they could read about throughout the Bible."

My point is that we should not turn the church into a tool for evangelism when, in reality, it should be a center for discipleship. The church's primary goal is to make disciples, like Jesus commanded. The fact that we have, in many ways, changed the purpose of the church by trying to make it a place to reach non-Christians means that the Christians who are coming to the church are not being made into productive disciples. They are not getting the food they need to grow and produce fruit. Another consequence is that, in many free churches, people are no longer speaking in tongues. The result is that new Christians are neither being baptized in the Holy Spirit nor receiving the gift of tongues because they do not see it put into practice. They might encounter tongues later in a cell group, but they are not likely to understand the importance of it because they did not receive it from the beginning. We see this in many Pentecostal churches today as well, and if they continue further down this road, there will be no "Pentecost" left in them!

We cannot put a lid on the movement of God's Spirit among us if we are going to be effective. Without God's Spirit, we can do nothing.

When Christians come together, they ought to be focused on pursuing God and being filled and equipped to live as disciples every day. Being a disciple means spreading the gospel, too, so that the fellowship can grow. This aspect is often overlooked when the church's focus is on reaching non-Christians. There are many dangers in using the church as a tool for evangelism instead of a center of discipleship the way the Bible says we should.

The idea of the church primarily being a place for non-Christians to come into relationship with Jesus can not be found in the Bible. This new way of having church has paved the way for what is now called the "seeker-friendly" church. As the word implies, it is a church that is designed to meet the newcomer. The focus is not removed just from equipping and training Christians, but many other important things also get changed in order to please the seekers (non-Christians), which is both incorrect as well as dangerous.

I understand why many pastors and leaders today have chosen this path. They long to see people come to Christ and are having a hard time seeing other possibilities for that to happen. They rarely see Christians doing the things I've talked about before, like inviting people into their homes and leading them to Christ. This is something that has been discussed in the church for many years, but we simply do not do it. Therefore, the pastor has to find other ways. It's much easier for Christians to invite non-Christians to a concert at church or to a seeker-friendly service than to invite them into their homes and share the gospel. Even the very thought can often create an immense fear in many Christians.

However, any way you look at it, in the end it is just an excuse for not doing what we should be doing, and it is the main reason for the lack of growth in the church. The reason for this is that the church has been transformed from a center for discipleship into a tool for evangelism. This has resulted in the fact that Christians simply are not being discipled anymore, and that makes it hard for them to reach people with the gospel. The church has not been trained how to do this, and most are filled with fear at even the thought of having to reach out to the world.

We have lost the capability to make disciples because of this change in the church's focus and purpose. Because the church is not growing anymore, pastors are getting desperate. However, instead of going back to the model we find in the Bible, church leaders are going down a totally different path. They are creating seeker-friendly churches and changing lots of things in order to get non-Christians into church. But this does not solve the problem. It actually does the opposite!!

With great sadness, I have to conclude that most free churches today are moving in this direction. They are focused on the wrong thing and are working hard to be more and more seeker-friendly all the time. By doing this, they might be getting more people to come to their church, but in the long run, they are not going to produce good and lasting fruit.

Remember, if we want to see whether a fellowship is healthy or not, we should not just look at the number of people attending. Instead, look to see whether the people are being made into disciples and followers of Jesus. This is not something that can be done on a Sunday morning when the fellowship meets for an hour and a half service. No, we get a better picture by looking at what the members of the fellowship are doing on Friday and Saturday nights and whether they are following Jesus' words each day. The purpose of the church is to make disciples that produce good fruit in their daily lives, and that is how we help the fellowship grow.

11

THE SEEKER-FRIENDLY CHURCH

The other day, I heard of a seeker-friendly church that removed the cross from a wall because it had provoked some of the people who visited. I think this paints a pretty good picture of the idea behind the seeker-friendly church. We have removed from the gospel that which offends people, with the hope that if we make the gospel more acceptable, non-Christians will want to come and meet with us. However, this means that Christians do not get the nutrition anymore that they need to grow.

If we take away the cross and that which offends the sinner, what then do we have left of the Gospel?

The church states that it is not the gospel message they are changing, but it is the "packaging" that must change. The truth of the matter is that we can wrap the message up so much that the salt loses its saltiness, and then we no longer even have the gospel. I personally do not think we should change the packaging; we should remove it altogether! Instead of spending so much time discussing what needs to be changed in order to get non-Christians to come in, we should be busy equipping Christians to go out and live the Christian life day in and day out. I believe that would solve the problem once and for all! And, again, all of this could happen if we simply began to fellowship like the first Christians did.

The gospel of Jesus Christ is not only God's power unto salvation, it is also a stumbling block. This is something Jesus said time and time again.

> Then He said to them all, "If anyone desires to come after Me, let him deny himself, and take up his cross daily, and follow Me. For whoever desires to save his life will lose it, but whoever loses his life for My sake will save it. For what profit is it to a man if he gains the whole world, and is himself destroyed or lost?" (Luke 9:23-25)

It is not popular today to say you have to deny yourself. It was not actually popular when Jesus said it either. Many times, the result was that people went away grieved or offended. However, Jesus did not turn around and run after them in order to compromise the truth or to try to package His message in a different way. One of the largest and most popular seeker-friendly churches in the USA made a survey of their members a while back.

This is what came out of that survey:

- 47% of the members did not believe they were saved by grace.
- 57% of the members did not believe in the Bible's authority.
- 56% of the members did not believe that Jesus is the only way to God.

Is this what we want to see happen in our churches right now? Again and again, I meet "Christians" who have no idea what the gospel is really about. They have gone to church for several years, but they do not live at all like disciples of Jesus.

Sadly, they did not ask how many of the members in the fellowship were truly disciples of Jesus and obeying Him each day, but that's what it's really all about. However, looking at these numbers, I can only imagine that the number would be very low. The survey gives a good picture of what might happen when we change the purpose of the church and turn it into an evangelistic tool rather than a center for discipleship.

In order to make the gospel attractive, we remove that which can bring salvation and actually change people. This will result in many people living in delusion and being lost.

Some time ago, I was contacted by a lady from Copenhagen. She listened to our teaching on baptism from the website "OplevJesus.dk" and wanted to be baptized. She had attended a seeker-friendly church for many years, but she never really understood baptism until she heard our teaching. The fact that this woman still did not understand the meaning of baptism worried me, especially because, according to the Bible, baptism is the entering into a new life in Christ. Nowadays, it has been exchanged for the prayer of salvation, for which we do not find any clear biblical evidence. Everyone who wanted to accept Jesus as their Lord was baptized at that moment, even if there were three thousand in one day or in the middle of the night. Some might say: "But what about the thief on the cross? He wasn't baptized."

It is true that he was not baptized, but the baptism of Jesus did not yet exist at that time. When the thief was hanging there on the cross, the old covenant was still in effect. Jesus was hanging beside the man. The baptism of Jesus symbolizes Jesus' death and resurrection, and that still had to take place when Jesus hung beside the thief on the cross. This is also the reason why we do not find anyone in the gospels being baptized with the baptism of Jesus. On the other hand, we do not find anyone after the crucifixion and resurrection of Jesus coming to faith and not being baptized at the same time. I do realize that baptizing people immediately after conversion is not very practical today with church programs where most churches have baptisms only once every three to six months, but we need to build our practice on the Bible and not our own traditions. This again shows how far we have actually strayed from the first church practices we read about in the Bible.

After the woman heard our teaching on baptism, she really wanted to hear more and came to one of our meetings. After my talk, she sat down and cried, saying she had never heard anything like it before, which is, in and of itself, frightening. I was simply preaching the gospel. I took her hands, and we prayed together. God's Spirit came over us in a strong way, and she immediately began speaking in tongues while we both cried. She opened her eyes and looked at me and quietly asked, "What am I doing?" I explained to her that she should simply continue, that she was speaking in tongues, and that it was the Holy Spirit who had come over her. She closed her eyes again and continued speaking in tongues. The next morning, she came to be baptized. She said that when she had gone home that evening, her daughter had come to her in pain. Some years ago, she had cut her hand on a window and still had a lot of pain. The mother had prayed for her many times, but nothing ever happened. When she arrived home that evening, her daughter came to her in pain. The mother put her hand on her and prayed, and this time it was as if the prayer came from her heart and not her head. Immediately, the daughter's pain disappeared.

After that, Lene and I visited the woman and her family. When I met the 13-year-old daughter, I asked her if she had been baptized in the Holy Spirit, and she answered no. People do not really talk about such things in seeker-friendly churches like the one they were involved in. Of course, she was still quite young, but she really wanted to be baptized in the Holy Spirit. To God, a 13-year-old girl is "old enough," so the girl's mother and I went into her room and prayed for her. The Holy Spirit came over her in a strong way, and she began speaking in tongues while she prayed and explained that she had never in her life felt so fantastic. Yes, God works just as powerfully in the room of a teenage girl as He does in a church. Later, the mother baptized her daughter herself with water in their bathtub. Since then, they have stopped attending the "seeker-friendly" church they had attended for many years and have started their own fellowship in their home, which no doubt is much more fulfilling.

They had attended one of the seeker-friendly churches that focused on having a large congregation, but we cannot let ourselves be fooled by the number of members a church has.

Seeker-friendly churches are most capable of getting people into their churches, and, of course, there are people who meet God there. I do not want to question that. However, I do hope that many of them will move on after a while in order to get closer to the Lord because, in most of these churches, they do not get the spiritual nutrition they need in order to grow. The concept of the seeker-friendly church simply creates difficulty in making disciples.

The problem here is not necessarily the fact that there is so much focus on those who are seeking. Setting the focus on those who are seeking is a good thing in and of itself. Personally, I try to reach out to non-Christians in different ways. For example, I will use language that non-Christians can understand. However, the problem lies in the fact that we have made the church into an evangelistic tool rather than a place where discipleship and mutual encouragement can take place. The church should be a place where Christians receive training in order to go boldly into the harvest fields.

Today, however, most Christians are not being equipped to go out and share the gospel. Instead, they are expecting the pastor to do everything. This creates an even bigger gap between the "professionals" who are active in ministry, and the majority of the people who simply sit in church and support them. In seeker-friendly churches, the world comes into the church, even though the church is called to be holy and set apart for God to equip people to go out and evangelize the world.

Several years ago at a Christian summer conference, the organizers arranged to hold a disco dance with a light show and smoke for the youngsters. They explained that they would begin the service with a time of worship to get people in the right frame of mind. After worship, the young people could dance and party with non-Christian music. This is yet another attempt to be a church where non-Christians can feel at home. As we have already seen many times before, the result will be backslidden and lukewarm young Christians.

Because of my extensive traveling, I have become increasingly aware of this danger over the last few years. I have the opportunity to meet many Christians from many different churches, and what I see worries me. I am very concerned about what the next generation of Christians will be like if we continue down this road.

This is what the Bible has to say about sin:

Flee also youthful lusts; but pursue righteousness, faith, love, peace with those who call on the Lord out of a pure heart. (2 Tim. 2:22)

We should flee from the things that might tempt us instead of letting temptations be served to us on a silver platter. To be relevant for non-Christians is not the same as being like the world in which they live. To be relevant is to separate oneself from the world and, instead, offer something that the world can not give them. The church is a gathering for Christians where they come together to build one another up. Then they can go out into the world again to display the life of Christ within them. This is something we should not change.

Non-Christian can, of course, be invited to a meeting. This works best in small groups where it is easier to discern the newcomer's need. This does not necessarily have to take the focus away from the equipping or training of the disciples. In fact, the opposite is quite true!

I am quite concerned that many will not see the problem until it is too late. In my country, many are so busy looking at megachurches in the USA that this message cannot be received enough to look honestly at the fruit they are producing. Jesus said that we should judge a tree by the quality of the fruit it produces and not only by the quantity.

> *"Beware of false prophets, who come to you in sheep's clothing, but inwardly they are ravenous wolves. You will know them by their fruits. Do men gather grapes from thornbushes or figs from thistles? Even so, every good tree bears good fruit, but a bad tree bears bad fruit. A good tree cannot bear bad fruit, nor can a bad tree bear good fruit."* (Matt. 7:15-18)

I believe there is a reason that seeker-friendly churches have been such a success in the USA and Denmark. It is because we do not experience the same opposition and persecution as Christians do in other parts of the earth. Unfortunately, because of this, we have not been able to see how things truly are. In the gospel of Mark, chapter four, Jesus uses an important parable about the sower:

> *And He said to them, "Do you not understand this parable? How then will you understand all the parables?"* (Mark 4:13)

The parable of the sower is the key to understanding the other parables. I am thinking in particular of the parables in the gospel of Matthew, chapter 25, the parables of the ten virgins, the ten talents, and the judgment of the world. These parables all tell of God's coming judgment. They warn that many will believe they had Jesus as their Lord when, in reality, they had never truly been born again.

In the parable about the judgment of the world, we can read that

Jesus will separate the sheep from the goats and not the sheep from the wolves as one might expect (Matthew 10:16). The judgment of the world deals with the people in the church who "confess" Jesus is Lord.

The parable of the sower describes different types of soil on which the seed falls. There is this one:

> *"Some fell on stony ground, where it did not have much earth; and immediately it sprang up because it had no depth of earth. But when the sun was up it was scorched, and because it had no root it withered away."* (Mark 4:5-6)

Here we see something grow up after the seed is sown. It looks really good in the beginning, and you can not see that anything is wrong with it. Someone hears the Word, comes to church, and is a "Christian" who "lives" with God. It looks like the plant is growing well, but something that you cannot see until the sun is high in the sky is very wrong with that seedling. Later, Jesus explains what the sun represents.

> *"These likewise are the ones sown on stony ground who, when they hear the word, immediately receive it with gladness; and they have no root in themselves, and so endure only for a time. Afterward, when tribulation or persecution arises for the word's sake, immediately they stumble."* (Mark 4:16-17)

The sun represents hardship and persecution that reveals the true condition of the heart. This can be a big problem in Denmark and the USA because we do not experience the same hardship and persecution as Christians do in many other countries. We may think we are growing as we should be, but much of the growth we see might not last simply because the Word of God has not taken root.

What would happen if we suddenly began experiencing persecution in Denmark, for example, the way Christians experience persecution in China?

I believe that, in that moment, it would become quite clear that the seeker-friendly church movement is only programs and procedures. I believe that, in a short amount of time, there would be few seeker-friendly churches left because most church-goers in the seeker-friendly churches would deny their faith as soon as being a Christian ceased to be fun and entertaining.

When the seed was sown in the stony ground, the message was heard and received with joy, just like we read in the parable. The message sounded so good that they accepted it with joy. Yet, we do not read that there is any grief involved over sin, and neither were they told about denying themselves and taking up their crosses. They heard and came to church faithfully, but the gospel never really took root in them. The truth is that we will not see this happen until the day the sun is at its highest point in the sky and everything gets revealed. Therefore, we should learn from the persecuted churches and listen to what they have to say. When we look at them, we do not see the same seeker-friendly ideas where the message is being nicely packaged and where people are drawn in with entertainment. When we read of the persecuted church, we find home fellowships that equip Christians to become disciples of Jesus, just like we read in the Bible. Also, as a matter of fact, these home fellowships grow many times faster than the seeker-friendly megachurches. We just do not hear about it because it is not being broadcasted on Christian TV channels.

Some argue that home fellowships exist because of persecution in certain parts of the world, and, because of that, they simply cannot have a "real" church. This is not true. The first church in the Bible also had periods of peace. However, during this time, they did not change the way they had fellowship. No, we only find home fellowships.

Remember, the question is not whether what we build can survive here and now but whether it can survive throughout eternity. I believe it is only a matter of time before persecution comes, and when it does, churches will be forced to change in order to survive. So why not make the necessary changes right now and build on the Rock? Then the house can stand when the waves come crashing against it.

12

What Is Church?

The word "church" occurs several times in the Bible. One place is, for example, 1 Corinthians.

And God has appointed these in the church: first apostles, second prophets, third teachers, after that miracles ... (1 Cor. 12:28)

In this chapter, we will take a closer look at the meaning of the word "church." Sometimes things can become confusing when people have different interpretations of the same word. As a result, I am often forced to use the word in a very clear way that leaves no room for wrong interpretation so that we do not misunderstand one another. I have done this in the previous chapters where I have talked about the church as a building to which we go. Now, however, I would like to take a closer look at the true meaning of the word "church."

The word we use for "church" that has been translated from the original language of the New Testament is: *ekklesia*. When we hear the word "church" today, the first thing that almost always comes to mind is a building. But the word *ekklesia* actually has no connection to a building or religion at all. The word simply means "an assembly or gathering."

In Acts, chapter 19, we read about the concerns of some people in Ephesus. Paul had preached the gospel and, as a result, some people became angry and began yelling, "Great is Diana of the Ephesians!" In verse 32, we read the following:

> *Some therefore cried one thing and some another, for the assembly was confused, and most of them did not know why they had come together.* (Acts 19:32)

We read in this passage that the assembly was confused, referring back to the assembly of non-Christians who worshipped the Goddess Diana. What is interesting is that the word used for "assembly" is the word *ekklesia*. So we could, in actuality, translate it like this: "Some therefore cried one thing and some another, for the *church* was confused, and most of them did not know why they had come together."

However, there is not really any point because we are reading about a group of Diana worshippers. When we hear the word "church," we get a picture in our head, and in the context we have just read, that picture is totally wrong! However, it is not only in this context that we have a problem; it's the fact that we have actually created a false picture in regard to the word "church." This passage proves that the word in the New Testament that we translate as "church" is not necessarily always referring to a Christian meeting or a building but simply to a gathering.

So the word *ekklesia* (which is mostly translated "church" in the Bible) really has nothing to do with a building or a religious meeting. *Ekklesia* means simply "an assembly of people." These people may be assembled on the street, in the home, or somewhere else. In the Bible, these assemblies often had to do with a gathering of Christians, and the word used for this gathering, *ekklesia*, was translated "church." Unfortunately, however, this also distorts the true meaning because, for us, "church" has come to mean much more than just a gathering of Christians. You probably would not consider an evening with Christian friends to eat and fellowship as having church, would you? However, that is, in fact, closer to the true meaning of the word "church" than if you were to say, "I'm just going down to the church to get something," and then you drove down to an empty building where you normally meet. This empty building has nothing at all to do with a gathering of people (church) because it's empty. The fact is that, today, we rather think of a building when we hear the word "church," even though that is kind of like calling a group of people a house. The two things have nothing to do with each other.

However, when seen through the eyes of the New Testament, there is actually no building that is holy! It is you and me—Christians—who are holy! If we meet at a particular place, it is not the place that is holy. When we leave that place, we are still holy, and the building is still only a building. God does not live in a building made of stone. No, He lives in us who live with Him. We are God's temple here on earth. Therefore, it does not matter where we meet. A gathering at McDonald's can be as holy as a meeting at St. Peter's Church.

Further, it does not matter if we meet together with only two or with two thousand. Jesus is in our midst in both occasions. Meeting in a building that is called a "church" does not make that meeting more significant than meeting on the street or in a house. Rather, the opposite is true because meeting on the street and in homes is actually what the first Christians did. The place where you gather has very little significance because of the fact that the word "church" merely means "an assembly" of Christians. Wherever a group of Christians meets, there we have, or are, the Church.

Around the year 300 A.D., the word "church" came into use, though we are not completely sure why. It is said that the word "church" comes from the Greek word *kuriakos,* which means "that which belongs to the Lord," or "the Lord's." This word, however, is only found in two places in the Bible, and neither of those places has anything to do with the church/assembly. In both places *kuriakos* is translated as "the Lord's."

I was in the Spirit on the Lord's [kuriakos] Day, and I heard behind me a loud voice, as of a trumpet … (Rev. 1:10)

Therefore when you come together in one place, it is not to eat the Lord's [kuriakos] Supper. (1 Cor. 11:20)

As you can see, we do not find the word "church" in the original language of the Bible. We actually do not even find the word "fellowship." Instead, we find the word "assembly" (*ekklesia*) over and over again.

Why, then, did we begin to use the word "church" instead of "assembly" if we do not find it in the Bible? The reason may be found in Emperor Constantine's worship of the sun god. At a certain point, he was even the high priest in the cult of the sun god (the Sol Invictus cult). If you search online for the word "church," you will find that "Church" (or Circe) is a sorceress from Greek mythology, the daughter of the sun god Helios and the moon goddess Perse."

This might explain why, during this time in history, the word "church" came into use. However, we do not know for sure. What we do know is that when our Bible uses the word "church" or "fellowship," it is translated from the word *ekklesia*, which simply means "assembly." So, when the Bible speaks of a "church" or "fellowship," it actually means "a gathering," and this gathering has nothing to do with a church building, membership, rules, Sunday services, etc.

When we begin to understand this, many things in the Bible will start to have a completely new meaning to us. So often, we have our own interpretation of things. Because of this, we often give a totally different interpretation of Scripture than what was originally written. This very thing has happened to the words "church" and "fellowship." If we try to use the word "assembly" instead, it may help us break away from the wrong associations we have with the word "church." Try it for yourself!! Forget everything about church buildings, rules, memberships, services, and whatever else you associate with the church. Then read the New Testament and put in the word "assembly" every time it says "church" or "fellowship," and you will understand what I mean.

Earlier, we read that God has given several gifts, or rather ministries, to the church. When we read this, most people think that God has put these ministries in a church building or a church network consisting of several churches. However, it does not refer to any particular church building, fellowship, or network. No, it refers to the assembly of believers in general. Firstly, the early Christians did not have any particular church organization. Secondly, they did not have a building that they called "church." When we read that God has given ministries to the church, it means He has given these to the assembly of believers in general, regardless of where they meet.

Let's read the passage again with a more accurate understanding:

[Among the assemblies of believers around and about in the home and on the streets, God has appointed some to be] ... first apostles,

second prophets, third teachers … (1 Cor. 12:28 [paraphrased])

When we begin to understand what different words really mean, it will start to give a whole new meaning to the Bible. You will start to understand how those first Christians really lived. It will give you the freedom to live with and serve God each day, no matter where you are. God comes out of the box we have put Him in, and Christianity today will again be like it was in the New Testament.

The church was an assembly of believers that met in both small and large groups. Their meetings had nothing to do with all the walls that we have built up today. There was no building or church organization with a name like Pentecostal, Baptist, or Lutheran. These are all walls we have put up and that God is going to break down in the last days. This will not happen by all the large church organizations becoming one and being put together in one big system. It will happen when church walls are broken down, and people once again begin to meet in homes and on the streets where there are no big names, programs, or organizations,. We will be led by the Spirit and what the Bible tells us we should believe and consider. The first Christians were not members of a church organization. They were simply representatives of Jesus Christ.

The separation we see between churches and believers today is the cause of many problems. One of these problems is that individual churches or organizations often miss out on what God wants to reveal to us through "the others." God gave me a vision of this some time ago.

The Bible says that we know in part, but one day we shall know God in full (1 Cor. 13). The idea of knowing in part is like all of us having our own bits of Christ. I have some bits of Him, and you have some bits of Him, etc., because God reveals different thing to each of us.

Today, we each sit in our own churches and groups, each with our own little bit of Jesus. But what would happen if we came together with all our bits and met at home? Yes, like a puzzle, we would be able to see more if we gathered the bits together. We would suddenly get a much bigger picture of who Christ actually is. When people today meet together for services, Christ is limited to what a single pastor knows about Him because the pastor is the only one who shares anything in these systems. The Bible, on the other hand, says that when we come together, everyone has something to share. This can only work in small assemblies. I have good friends in different church organizations, friends who really love Jesus and are my brothers in the Lord. We can meet freely and share the Word, even though there are still some areas where we see things a little differently. We are adjusting to each other a little every time we meet. This is a great blessing because in such a gathering we see other parts of Jesus that we would not see otherwise. This gives a bigger revelation of the Bible and Who Jesus is. This, however, could never happen in the same way in churches where people are being warned against "the others" and where the members are being imprisoned because of the church's fear of losing them. If we are to become one, it needs to happen on a personal level. It is simple if we take away the walls that have been built by our organizations. The individual first needs to be one with Christ, and then we can easily be one with each other.

You are Christ's church here on earth. This is who you are twenty-four hours a day, seven days a week! If you meet someone from another church, you should be allowed to share Christ with one another because you are part of the same body/church. When you come together, you are the church, and you can, therefore, share Christ and be a blessing and an encouragement to each other. This is how it should be. Unfortunately, it is not always this way. Many feel today that we should not "touch one another's sheep."

I truly believe in unity, but a unity that is built on Jesus Christ, not on a church system or structure. There was not any membership in the first assemblies either. When one repented and was baptized, they were baptized into the body of Christ. They belonged to Christ and not any particular church or organization. Therefore, they could easily have meetings with others who also belonged to Christ. You were not a member of any one church and, thus, not a part of any man's vision. There was no fear or competition involved when believers came together.

The first fellowships consisted of many small independent groups that simply related to each other in love. There was no church denomination, competition, or control. These fellowships could be small, consisting of only two or three people, or they could be bigger, with twenty or thirty people. There often was an exchange between them. New people would come in, and new groups were being started, or they would split up into different groups. They were together often, and it was like a small family that grew. It was not about where they met, membership, or how many there were. It was about meeting and sharing Christ in such a way that everyone could put their "little bit" into the fellowship. They often ate together, and communion was a regular part of that Love feast.

"For where two or three are gathered together in My name, I am there in the midst of them." (Matt. 18:20)

Because they met in smaller groups, they naturally became like a family, coming together daily and sharing life. During my almost two decades as a Christian, I have been in various churches, but I have to say that only in these last few years have I truly experienced the church as my family. I can say that I love the people with whom I meet. It is love and Christ that hold us together, not a building or a membership. This is something I really want others to experience as well.

13

YOU ARE THE CHURCH

The church is not a building or a place where you can visit. You are the church! You are Christ's body here on earth. You are the church wherever you are and wherever you go. The fact that we are Christ's body is something I believe most Christians have heard before, but only a few are living that way.

One of the problems with having a church building is that we easily start to see the church building as a more "holy" place than other places. Furthermore, a church building tends to have an effect on our behavior and attitude, where we start to reduce the Christian life to something "we do" at a specific time and at a specific place. I'm not saying that this is always the case, but the risk is surely there. It just so happens that there are people today who act, say, and do things at home and at other places that they would never think of doing at church. To them, their everyday life is different compared to their life in church, especially on Sunday mornings. Church is seen as the place where God is and where we, therefore, need to act correctly.

This, however, was never God's intent, and it is exactly what Jesus did away with in the New Covenant.

"Our fathers worshiped on this mountain, and you Jews say that in Jerusalem is the place where one ought to worship." Jesus said to her, "Woman, believe Me, the hour is coming when you will neither on

*this mountain, nor in Jerusalem, worship the Father. You worship
what you do not know; we know what we worship, for salvation is of
the Jews. But the hour is coming, and now is, when the true
worshipers will worship the Father in spirit and truth; for the Father
is seeking such to worship Him. God is Spirit, and those who worship
Him must worship in spirit and truth." The woman said to Him, "I
know that Messiah is coming" (who is called Christ). "When He
comes, He will tell us all things."* (John 4:20-24)

Jesus came to make a new and better covenant. He came to build
himself a "house" out of you and me. God wants to live in us, and this
means 24 hours a day, 7 days a week. There is not anything that
happens at church on Sundays that cannot happen at home every day.
When we understand this and seriously start to include God in our
everyday lives, our lives will never be the same again. However, many
are living an everyday life that is completely different from the one they
are living at church on a Sunday morning when they come together to
worship. Many of them are deceiving themselves by believing that
everything is okay as long as they come to church on Sunday.

Life with God encompasses every day, every minute of a Christian's
life, and every place we go. It is not something we do now and then at
a certain time and place. It does not necessarily belong to one special
place. There are, of course, occasions when we give Him full attention
above all else. Even when the attention is on other things God never
disappears.

Is it possible to experience God as a part of everyday life in the
same way we do when we are going to church on Sundays?

Yes, of course, it is possible! Life with God, however, often gets
reduced to something that only takes place at a certain location (church
building), at a special time (church service on a Sunday morning),
when a particular person (the pastor) does certain things that we are
told only he can do (communion and sermon).

Research from the USA has shown that only ten percent of those
regularly going to church talk with each other and their children about
God daily. That might indicate that ninety percent of those attending
church are not living with God in their everyday lives. This should
bother us when we realize that, from the beginning of creation, God

primarily meant for the Christian life to be part of the family and the everyday life. Many people, however, seem to substitute this with their weekly attendance of a church.

We see the same thing happen with the idea of Sunday school. The first Sunday school came about at the end of the 18th century in Europe. When it came to the USA in the beginning of the 19th century, many big churches were actually against it. They did not want to have it in their churches. This is hard to imagine for many of us. Why in the world did they not want a Sunday school in their churches? There is not anything wrong with Sunday schools, is there? The reason for this was that they feared a Sunday school would start to take the place of those to whom God had given the responsibility to teach children about Him, such as parents, and especially fathers who are the priests in the home.

When we look at churches today, we have to conclude that the American churches were right in their concern. Sunday schools have, in many places, replaced the parents' responsibility for teaching their children. Only ten percent of those who go to church talk with their children about God daily. This means that only a very small portion of Christians nowadays are teaching their children God's Word!

The main reason for this is that many today think teaching their children about God is something the Sunday school will take care of. We have handed the responsibility over to a system that we do not even find in the Bible. Sunday school in itself is not wrong, but it should never lead us to hand over a responsibility that God has given to parents.

In the same way, the church has often become a replacement for one's own personal life with God. Many are thinking, "It's the priest's job to hear from God and teach me," and "It's the responsibility of the church to see that I grow in my walk with God," etc. The responsibility for one's own personal life with God has been relegated to a system where it does not belong. Again, I want to underline that it is not necessarily this way everywhere, but if we are not careful, this is what easily may happen.

When we take another look at the idea of church, we will realize that we are the only real church building that God has. We are God's temple (church) here on earth, according to His Word.

Do you not know that you are the temple of God and that the Spirit of God dwells in you? (1 Cor. 3:16)

Or do you not know that your body is the temple of the Holy Spirit who is in you, whom you have from God, and you are not your own? For you were bought at a price; therefore glorify God in your body and in your spirit, which are God's. (1 Cor. 6:19-20)

We are God's temple, and it is the only temple He has. We should, therefore, honor God with our bodies, which, as I said earlier, is something that applies seven days a week. We are God's temple, and we are all priests as well.

… from Jesus Christ, the faithful witness, the firstborn from the dead, and the ruler over the kings of the earth. To Him who loved us and washed us from our sins in His own blood, and has made us kings and priests to His God and Father, to Him be glory and dominion forever and ever. Amen. (Rev. 1:5-6)

This is our position today under the New Covenant. Today, we are God's temple, and all of us are priests. Or, to be more specific, you are God's church, and you are a priest with personal access to God. The only thing holy about a church building and a church meeting is you and others who are attending there. You have access to the holy of holies because of Jesus' precious blood, if you are born again and are living with Him. We do not need a high priest as a middleman anymore, like we read about in the Old Testament. We do not necessarily need to go to a specific church building or have a "real" priest in order to have a church service. We are all priests and can all hear from God, baptize people, hand out communion, pray for the sick, etc. You are the church, and you are the priest. The service actually has to do with you as well. If you search for the word "service" in the Danish Bible, it comes up in only two places. One of them is the following:

I beseech you therefore, brethren, by the mercies of God, that you present your bodies a living sacrifice, holy, acceptable to God, which is your reasonable service. (Romans 12:1)

A service is not only something physical with special rituals like we see today. This verse explains very well what a service really is. It is not necessarily a special meeting at a specific time and place. Rather, it is a lifestyle in which we offer our bodies (as God's temple) to God, so that He can live in and through us. We are the sacrifice, so He can make His home in us and use us for His purpose.

We have reduced the church to a building or a place, but, in reality, the church is a certain person; that is to say: you! The pastor has also become a person with the responsibility to do things for you that you should be doing yourself because, today, you yourself are a priest before God. In the same way, our idea of service has become something that only happens at a certain place and a certain time, usually Sunday mornings. However, true service takes place when each of us uses our own body to worship God, and that is something that can happen whenever and wherever two or three are together. The strong spiritual life that the first Christians lived is strongly related to their understanding of these things. When you realize this, it will lead you into even more freedom with God.

14

CHURCH SERVICE

W hen we look at the different types of church services that
exist today, we find that, wherever we look, they almost all
look the same. In the Catholic Church, communion is put
at the center of the service. The Catholic Church believes that the bread
and wine are not just symbols but that they actually do become the
physical body and blood of Jesus during communion. This idea goes all
the way back to Gregory the Great (540-604 A.D.). Luther fought against
this idea, however, so that, today, we have the Lutheran service where
the preacher is placed in the center of the service. This actually laid the
foundation for the Protestant and the Lutheran church tradition. Today,
in most churches, communion, the pulpit, and the preacher are still the
most important elements in the church service. Another big change that
came with the Protestant and Lutheran tradition was the idea of whole
congregations singing together during the church service, which did
not happen in the Catholic churches of those days. Besides these
elements, there is not any big difference between that which Gregory
the Great presented during the 6th century and that which Luther
presented during the 16th century.

If we look at the services in the average free churches today, we will
not find much difference in the way the services are conducted there
either. There are, of course, small differences in the way things are
presented, but the structure is very much the same as it was back then.

In a typical free church, you start with a welcome, then prayer, and after that some worship songs. Then there will be announcements and a collection, a couple more songs, and then the preacher gets up to preach. When the sermon, which is always a one way communication, is finished, then it is time for prayer. In some places, communion is performed right after the sermon. Finally, the morning is finished off with church coffee. This structure reminds me very much of the structure of church services in the more traditional churches. Such church services are usually conducted by a worship leader and a preacher. Most of the time, the pastor/preacher is also the person leading the meeting. The rest of the fellowship can join in with the songs, but, other than that, they have to be satisfied with what all of the other "participants" are doing. If someone were to ask you on Monday if it was a good service, you would mostly consider what you thought of the preacher, the sermon, and perhaps the worship. But let's look at what the Bible says about "church service."

> *How is it then, brethren? Whenever you come together, each of you has a psalm, has a teaching, has a tongue, has a revelation, has an interpretation. Let all things be done for edification.* (1 Cor. 14:26)

The important thing to understand here is that Paul is saying "when you come together, each of you has something to contribute for edification." The list shown here is not the most important part because it could surely be longer. Paul is teaching that, when we come together, each of us should bring something that can be used to edify, build up, or encourage each other. But in a typical free-church service today, only three or four people normally bring something. The rest of the people just sit there with their "bit" of Christ. The bigger the church, the more people are sitting there passively. Yes, some will argue that if everyone got to talk for any length of time, it would become a horribly long service, and I agree. The only reason this would not work today is that we simply have too many people in our meetings. What we see in the Bible is that the first Christians met in small house groups, and not in big church meetings. In these smaller groups, it would not necessarily take a very long time for everyone to share a word, testimony, or a song.

The Bible verse that we just read is actually the only reference to the structure of church meetings that we find in the New Testament. There is no biblical evidence for a service with a specific order like welcome, songs, collection, and preaching. We also do not find any biblical reference to the idea that only a few should be sharing, with the rest sitting and listening. We do read in the Bible about one event where Paul talked the whole night (Acts 20), but I do not believe this was a long, unbroken sermon by Paul. I believe he talked that long because the other people were taking part in it, too.

If we look at the original text, we find in Acts, chapter 20 two different words that are both translated to the same word. One of them means "speech" or to "talk." The other word, however, does not have to do with speaking but with leading a dialog or conversation. So Paul probably talked for part of the time, and after he spoke, they had active dialog that lasted into the night. The whole group was involved in asking questions that directed the conversation. This event was nothing like we see today, where one person talks for 45 minutes without interruption, and then they give a thank you and dismiss.

If we look at the way the early Christians met, it is completely different from how we meet today. First of all, they did not have a church building. Second, they did not have a church service every Sunday. And third, they did not have the structure in their meetings that we have today. Instead, they met in homes and shared Christ with each other. They ate together and shared communion as a part of a normal mealtime. After they ate, they all had the opportunity to share something to edify the others. Some people might have come with a vision or a song, and some others with a passage from God's Word or an experience that they had. This way of meeting has different effects on the people. First, it means that everyone has a bigger picture of who Christ is because this picture is no longer limited to the revelation of the pastor and only a few others. It also means that people are not so easily frustrated anymore because they have a chance to talk about what they have experienced. Furthermore, it means that people will grow in a totally different way.

When we look at free churches today we see different groups of Christians. There is a very small group of people who are actively serving in the church and are satisfied; they have found a place in the church where they can serve God. They feel like they're being used and are growing because of it. They are satisfied and feel no need for change. Unfortunately, this group is very small. The other group is very big. First of all, there are many who are dissatisfied and frustrated because they are not being used and are not growing in the things that God has put in them. These people have sat in church for many years and listened, Sunday after Sunday. Some begin to criticize everyone and everything out of pure frustration. These people have chosen to put their dreams on the shelf and to accept the fact that they can not grow or be used any further. They have been beaten down; the fire inside has slowly gone out, and they have finally become complacent, lukewarm, and possibly even backslidden. They continue to come to church, but in their hearts, they have already left their first love and lost their fire.

We need to see a reformation in our church structure. If you remember, we really wanted to do something different when we were planning our first church service some years ago. But what happened? It became exactly like the ones we had left. The truth is that church tradition lies deep within all of us. It takes a long time for this to change, but with God's help it can happen.

> *I beseech you therefore, brethren, by the mercies of God, that you present your bodies a living sacrifice, holy, acceptable to God, which is your reasonable service. And do not be conformed to this world, but be transformed by the renewing of your mind, that you may prove what is that good and acceptable and perfect will of God.* (Romans 12:1-2)

Most people who read this think of sin and wrong thoughts. But this Scripture does not only refer to sin and wrong thoughts, it also has to do with the determination not to adjust to the systems of this world. We should not follow the ideas that don't exist in the Bible and that aren't connected to Christ. We should renew our minds so that we can do what God wants us to do. Don't follow the traditions and systems that are built on the world's philosophy and on religion. Let your mind be renewed so that you can understand how God wants His church to function and also what He wants you to do to make disciples.

15

THE POWER OF EXAMPLE

We stated earlier that Jesus has called us to make people into His disciples. I believe we are wrong when we think this will happen all by itself or simply by people attending our church meetings Sunday after Sunday. Listening to teachings does not necessarily make one into a disciple.

Jesus was a carpenter, but He did not build a single church! He never started an organization, nor did he have church services at any specific time. Neither did He start a Bible school to get the job done. No, the way He made disciples was entirely different from the way in which we do it today. In chapter four of the gospel of Matthew, we read about Jesus calling His first disciples.

> And Jesus, walking by the Sea of Galilee, saw two brothers, Simon called Peter, and Andrew his brother, casting a net into the sea; for they were fishermen. Then He said to them, "Follow Me, and I will make you fishers of men." They immediately left their nets and followed Him. (Matt. 4:18-20)

Jesus called his disciples with the words: "Follow Me." A disciple of Jesus was, and still is, a follower of Jesus. We leave what we are doing behind in order to follow Him. Yet, what did Jesus do to make people into His disciples? Did He build a church where they could meet every

Sunday? Did He start a Bible school where He could meet the students every morning and teach them?

In the *Everyday Danish Bible* there is an explanation of the verses that we just read. It says this:

> "In those days teaching often involved following a master and learning from His example. A disciple is rather an apprentice than a student. That is why the disciples and other people often called Jesus *master*."

There are many truths hidden in what we have just read. In the culture in which Jesus and the first Christians lived, things were done very differently than what we do in our various cultures today. Being taught by someone, then, meant following a master. However, following the master did not mean that you learned by sitting and listening only, but by seeing and doing. It was both teaching and learning by example.

Today, almost all learning in the church happens by listening to someone teaching. What makes you a student is mostly sitting and listening to the teachings. It is actually the way our whole society functions. Fortunately, more and more schools are beginning to introduce new ways of learning. They are beginning to involve the kids so that they are not just listening but are more actively involved. Research on how people learn most effectively reveals the following:

We remember:
  10% of what we read,
  20% of what we hear,
  30% of what we see,
  50% of what we hear and see,
  70% of what we say ourselves,
  90% of what we do ourselves.

As you can see, there is a big difference in what we learn between simply sitting and listening, which is what we do most in churches, and talking, seeing, and doing.

Jesus taught his disciples by having them follow Him. In that way they did not just experience what He taught, but they also saw how He lived. After they had watched how He did things, Jesus sent them out to do what He had shown them. This is an important part of learning that is, unfortunately, often left out today.

The way teaching is done in churches nowadays easily creates a distant relationship between the common church visitor and the pastor or speaker, and that's exactly what it felt like when I was a new Christian. Because of this distance, people often do not grow in their faith.

Nowadays, when I am out in the country, I often meet people who have respect for me because of my ministry. It is one thing to have respect for me based on what they see of me on my website or a couple of times each year in a pulpit, but it is something completely different when you talk to me and meet me in the different situations of everyday life. Those who hear me teach only remember twenty percent of what I say. The people who talk to me each day grow in a completely different way, especially when I am taking them out to practice what they have learned.

They are not only taught through my words but also through my way of life. They are not only listening, but they are also learning by seeing how I treat my wife and my children, how I think about others, and how I spend my time with God, etc. They learn by following me and doing what I do. The church is supposed to be a part of everyday life, not something that only takes place in a certain place for a couple of hours each week.

When you consider that most of what we learn actually happens by seeing how others do it, what is it then that we are learning in many of our churches today? Do you learn how to give a testimony? Do you learn how to be a good father or a good husband? No, this is something that is learned in everyday life and not something that can be taught in two hours sitting in a church on a Sunday morning. Of course, we can be taught by listening to a sermon, but it is still not teaching by example. What we do learn in church is how people teach, sing songs, welcome others, and many other things that belong to church life.

God has not, however, called us to be "professional" Christians living a "professional" church life. We are called to go out and make disciples of all nations every day, disciples who are living the life each day. God has not called us to serve Him only in some small areas of our lives, leaving the rest alone. Being successful in a speaker's chair while the family is falling apart is not being successful at all. No, it is about your entire life. That is why Jesus called people to follow Him, so that, through life's challenges, they would learn by example.

A good picture of the way Jesus and the first Christians lived is that of an apprentice and his master. It is a practice that does not occur as much today as it did some years ago. The thought behind this practice is that the student (apprentice) learns from an experienced teacher (master) by following his example until he becomes experienced and competent himself. How did such an apprentice learn? Well, first of all by seeing what his master did. In teaching this way, the apprentice not only learned by seeing, but also by hearing and doing.

After some time, the apprentice will start trying to do things on his own. However, the master will stay by his side to see how he is doing and to help when and where it's needed. After a while, the apprentice will begin to do things on his own more and more until, finally, he is fully educated and able to move on. With the Christian life, it should actually be the same. We follow other mature Christians and learn from their example. After a short time, we will be ready to perform tasks and teach others ourselves.

"A disciple is not above his teacher, but everyone who is perfectly trained will be like his teacher." (Luke 6:40)

In the gospel of Luke, chapter nine, you can read another example of how Jesus taught His disciples. Here, He gives them an order along with some practical instructions. It says, among other things:

He sent them to preach the kingdom of God and to heal the sick. And He said to them, "Take nothing for the journey, neither staffs nor bag nor bread nor money; and do not have two tunics apiece. Whatever house you enter, stay there, and from there depart." (Luke 9:2-4)

Everything Jesus is saying to His disciples here is meant for them to learn something specific. Later, we read:

And He said to them, "When I sent you without money bag, knapsack, and sandals, did you lack anything?" So they said, "Nothing." Then He said to them, "But now, he who has a money bag, let him take it, and likewise a knapsack; and he who has no sword, let him sell his garment and buy one. For I say to you that this which is written must still be accomplished in Me: 'And He was numbered with the transgressors.' For the things concerning Me have an end." (Luke 22:35-37)

Jesus sent them out at this specific time so they would learn something specific: to trust God. Later when Jesus said, "As the Father has sent Me, I am also sending you" (John 20:21), His disciples knew what this meant. They had seen how He had been sent out by the Father. Jesus was with His disciples for only three years, but it was enough for them to then go out and change the world.

Today, we see Christians sitting in church pews for 15 or 20 years without any big changes. Why? Could the reason be that we have built up a church system that is not capable of training people through example? Could the reason be that one remembers only twenty percent of what one hears?

Imagine a young man who really wants to become an electrician. Of course, he begins by sitting on a school bench listening to a teacher and reading books. But the funny thing is that, after four years, he still has not actually done anything himself. He has just listened and read without applying his knowledge in any practical way. He has read all the books and heard all the teachings on how this is a redundant statement: it should be done. He knows everything about it. But now the time has come for him to show what he has learned during those four years. What do you think is going to happen? Yes, he is probably going to be afraid, nervous, insecure, and will have difficulty remembering all that he has heard and read. He is going to think: "What am I supposed to do now? It's not like what I heard and read. What if something goes wrong?" He's probably going to turn back because he realizes the gap between the theory and real life is simply too big.

Fortunately, this is probably never going to happen to an electrician today. In reality, as a student, he is going to be trying things all the time, and a lot of the lessons will include practical training. After a short time in school, he will begin an internship where he will work beside someone with more experience until he is finally ready to go and work by himself.

The only place where we actually do not learn this way today is in our churches. In our churches today, we simply listen and read, without ever gaining the experience of practical application. This is why we have a church that is filled with fear and that will never go out into the real world and do what Jesus has commanded us to do. We know all about how to do it, but we just can not seem to actually do it ourselves.

Let's look at an example: Someone comes to me who really wants to hear about God, and I place him with a Christian who has been attending church regularly for ten years. I charge the Christian: "Will you explain the gospel to this person? If he repents, baptize him in water and with the Holy Spirit, and then disciple him." What do you think would happen? I think the Christian would not know what to do. A true and trained disciple of Jesus, however, would gladly make the other into a disciple because this is part of the mission Jesus has given us.

Today, there is a huge spirit of fear standing between the church and the world. We can only take it away by beginning to make people into disciples on a daily basis like Jesus taught us.

Look at Christians who have been sitting in the church for ten or fifteen years. Ask yourself whether they are able to do what I have been talking about. If the answer is no, you know that they are not going to be able to do it in the future either; that is, if they continue in the same way for another ten or fifteen years. We are often so gullible and think that if we continue a little while longer in the same way, things are going to change. I am convinced that, if change does not happen now, it is not going to happen in the future by continuing to do the same things over and over again.

When we realize that we learn mostly by example, we will understand that it is incredibly important who we hang out with. The truth is, we do not learn most things from listening to the preachers in the church. We are actually influenced more by others we meet in the church and everyone else we relate to in everyday life. It is like the story of a duckling that opens its eyes for the first time. It thinks that the first thing it sees is its mother. In the same way, when you are born again and your spiritual eyes are opened, the Christianity you see around you is going to be "real" and "normal." Of course, this can be changed, but that is not so easy.

If you become part of a fellowship where many are living in sin, there is a big risk that you will start to do the same. If, instead, you become part of a fellowship where people are on fire for the Lord and serve Him in word and deed, then, in the same way, you will probably be set on fire for Him. The truth is that we learn through what we see and experience around us, and we tend to adapt to our surroundings.

It is so important to build relationships with people who are true, burning disciples for Jesus. In the first fellowships, you could not just walk in from the street and become a part of the fellowship. There had to be evidence that you had really repented and were living right before the Lord. The Bible makes it clear that this should still be the same today. We should remove evil from our midst because a little leaven affects the whole lump (1 Cor. 5:6).

> *But now I have written to you not to keep company with anyone named a brother, who is sexually immoral, or covetous, or an idolater, or a reviler, or a drunkard, or an extortioner—not even to eat with such a person. For what have I to do with judging those also who are outside? Do you not judge those who are inside? But those who are outside God judges. Therefore "put away from yourselves the evil person." (1 Cor. 5:11-13)*

This is incredibly important. Again and again, I am astonished at how new Christians grow when they are in a fellowship where people love Jesus with all of their hearts. I have seen people going into the streets evangelizing and praying for the sick, people from whom I would never have expected this based on their personality. However, after they had come into a fellowship where many were doing just that, it became natural for them to do the same. What we see of "Christianity" in the beginning is what we're going to see as normal. So we have to begin creating fellowships where we really serve Jesus in word and deed. This way, we will learn by what we see around us and truly influence the people with whom we associate.

16

THE TWO MIRRORS

The Bible speaks of two mirrors, or actually, of two different ways of looking into a mirror. We read about one way in the second letter to the Corinthians:

But we all, with unveiled face, beholding as in a mirror the glory of the Lord, are being transformed into the same image from glory to glory, just as by the Spirit of the Lord. (2 Cor. 3:18)

In this example, the Word of God is being compared to a mirror. By reading God's Word, we are transformed into the very image we see in it, the very image of which it speaks. There is, however, another example in the Word of God concerning the way we look into a mirror. This example is found in the letter of James:

But be doers of the word, and not hearers only, deceiving yourselves. For if anyone is a hearer of the word and not a doer, he is like a man observing his natural face in a mirror; for he observes himself, goes away, and immediately forgets what kind of man he was. But he who looks into the perfect law of liberty and continues in it, and is not a forgetful hearer but a doer of the Word, this one will be blessed in what he does. (James 1:22-25)

In the second example we again see the Word of God being likened to a mirror. However, unlike the first example where the person looking into the mirror was being transformed from glory to glory, we read here about someone who looks into a mirror, but as soon as he turns away from it, he forgets what he saw. What is the difference between these two people? Why is the one person being changed into that which he has heard, while the other only hears the Word and does not change. The answer is found in verse 25:

> *But he who looks into the perfect law of liberty and continues in it, and is not a forgetful hearer but a doer of the Word, this one will be blessed in what he does.* (James 1:25)

These Scriptures clearly illustrate one of the main problems that the church is facing today: our churches are built around the idea that teaching in itself can change people! However, teaching in and of itself is powerless if we do not act on what we've heard. We are not blessed, or changed, through what we hear but through what we do with what we hear! Many Christians are sitting in church Sunday after Sunday, year after year, listening to teachings, but there is no sign of any significant change in their lives. They have come to believe that if they just keep coming to church and keep listening to the right teachings, something will begin to happen in their life. However, that is a lie! James wrote right here that we deceive ourselves if we do not act on what we hear. We deceive ourselves when what we hear does not really change us. We might come to church faithfully every Sunday, but when we leave, we immediately forget what we have just heard. When we are asked a week later whether it was a good service or not, we say yes, but when asked what he talked about, we do not remember.

In order for us to be blessed and for our lives to truly be changed, it is not enough to just hear the Word. We are blessed only when we become doers of the Word. If we believe teaching alone is going to change us, then we are deceiving ourselves. When we listen to a teaching without acting on it, we are like the one who looked at himself in a mirror but immediately forgot what he looked like. We hear a message, but as soon as we leave the service, we have forgotten it.

If I had never left the church I was in, I most likely would not have come to where I am today. I am not saying that I was not taught well in that church because I was, but the whole system made it unbelievably difficult for me to act on what I heard. Imagine that we are sitting in a church, and we hear something we know we should go out and put into practice. However, the moment you step through those church doors into the big wide world, you find that you are totally alone in this, and suddenly, it is difficult. We are like the apprentice who only spent time in school and never practiced what he learned. That is why we must go back to the way Jesus did things, to say, "Come and follow Me." "Come and see what I'm doing, and start to do the same while I am standing by your side."

I have thought for many years that people in the church should pull themselves together and begin living out the Christian life on a daily basis. I have realized, however, that this is actually very difficult to do as long as we continue doing church the way many do today. Since we began working with small house groups, we have seen people grow like never before. New converts quickly grow to the level of people who have gone to church for many years. I have seen new converts, having been saved for only a few weeks, lead people to Christ, baptize them in water, and pray with them for the baptism of the Spirit. I have seen Christians, after just a few months of being saved, sharing the Word with both Christians and non-Christians as if they had been going to church for many years. They have grown so fast because of the example of others. I will ask again: "How many people do we know who have gone to church for ten or fifteen years who still can not share the Word, baptize in water, and pray for the baptism of the Spirit? How many do we know who, after ten or fifteen years, still need milk (Hebrews 5:11-14) from others because they cannot feed themselves?"

We can continue having services the same way for the next ten or fifteen years without seeing any change, but if we want to grow and see others grow as well, we must change the way we run the church. We want to build our lives on the Rock. We cannot just hear the Word, but we need to act on it like Jesus was saying in the parable of the wise and foolish builders. Notice that, in this parable, the difference is not in what they hear but in what they do.

"Therefore whoever hears these sayings of Mine, and does them, I will liken him to a wise man who built his house on the rock: and the rain

descended, the floods came, and the winds blew and beat on that house; and it did not fall, for it was founded on the rock. But everyone who hears these sayings of Mine, and does not do them, will be like a foolish man who built his house on the sand: and the rain descended, the floods came, and the winds blew and beat on that house; and it fell. And great was its fall." (Matt. 7:24-27)

The Bible supports what the research shows. We change and learn best through what we do. The following is worth repeating.

We remember:
    10% of what we read
    20% of what we hear
    30% of what we see
    50% of what we hear and see
    70% of what we say ourselves
    90% of what we ourselves do.

When I teach, I hope the listener will get something out of what I'm sharing. I hope you will get something out of reading this book. It is doubtful, however, that you will get as much out of this book as I do. According to the researchers, when I teach, those listening to me will remember twenty percent of what I have said. But for me, as the teacher, it is entirely different. I go and pray about what I am going to share. I meditate on it, study about it, and when it has really become a part of me, I go and speak about it. This means that I get so much more out of it than those who are listening. Everyone who has tried to teach knows what I'm talking about. It takes a lot more to speak about something yourself than to just listen to someone else speak.

Therefore, we need to create a "platform" where everyone has the opportunity to share something, not just for the "listeners" sake, but for the sake of those speaking.

When I want to encourage a Christian to read more in the Bible and learn more this week than he did last week, I will ask him to share something in the next gathering. Because of this, he will seek God, dig deep in the Word, read and study, in order to have something to share. When he has found a topic, he will start thinking and meditating on it until the time comes for him to share it. The next day, if I were to ask those who were listening what they remember, they are bound to have remembered something. However, if I were to ask him, he would be able to tell the entire message all over again. This is one of the reasons why I believe in small gatherings and fellowships where *everyone* has the opportunity to share something—just like in the first fellowships.

17

EQUIPPED FOR MINISTRY

After Jesus was taken up into heaven, the Christians continued with Jesus' method of teaching. The gifts that Jesus had were divided among the fellowship so that even today we can function as Christ's body here on earth.

> *And He Himself gave some to be apostles, some prophets, some evangelists, and some pastors and teachers, for the equipping of the saints for the work of ministry, for the edifying of the body of Christ, till we all come to the unity of the faith and of the knowledge of the Son of God, to a perfect man, to the measure of the stature of the fullness of Christ; that we should no longer be children, tossed to and fro and carried about with every wind of doctrine, by the trickery of men, in the cunning craftiness of deceitful plotting ... (Eph. 4:11-14)*

Here we read about the offices that Jesus passed down to us. We call these offices (apostles, prophets, evangelists, pastors, and teachers) the five-fold ministry. The purpose of the five-fold ministry is to equip the holy ones to serve, just like we read.

An evangelist's purpose is not just to go out on the street and proclaim the gospel. No, his primary task is to equip the believers to evangelize and to serve. The same goes for the teacher. A teacher's task is not only to teach believers, but also to train up believers to break down and share the Word themselves. It is so important for us to get this straight; otherwise, the fellowship is not going to grow as it should.

Many people today have the wrong belief that the purpose of an evangelist is to go out and proclaim the gospel so that other Christians do not need to do so. Many believe that teachers should teach so that we do not need to read God's Word for ourselves, and prophets should prophesy so that we do not need to listen to God ourselves. This is not at all what the New Testament teaches us.

It is true that not everyone is called to be an evangelist, a teacher, a prophet, etc., but every Christian should learn how to share Christ, teach others, prophesy, etc. This is part of the ministry that everyone has received. The five-fold ministry has been placed in the church to equip the saints so that *they* can do the work of the ministry. To serve means, first and foremost, that we are sent out into the earth as representatives of Christ (2 Cor. 5:20). When we are Jesus' disciples, we live with Him every day.

> *And God has appointed these in the church: first apostles, second prophets, third teachers, after that miracles, then gifts of healings, helps, administrations, varieties of tongues.* (1 Cor. 12:28)

Here it is again, a list of some of the services that God has put in the church. Let me give an example of how this can work today.

- *Are all evangelists?* No.
- *Can all evangelize and share Jesus with each other?* Yes!

- *Has everyone the gift of healing?* No.
- *Can everyone, according to the Bible, pray for the sick, and they can be healed?* Yes!

- *How then does this function?*

For an example, I work as an evangelist and have the gift of healing the sick, but the reason why God has given me this gift is not so everyone can see me on a platform proclaiming the gospel and healing the sick. This might be part of what it means to be an evangelist, but it is not my primary role. I have been given to the fellowship to equip the saints with the gifts that God has given me. In the house fellowships of which we have been a part, about ninety percent of the people share Jesus on a daily basis. The same goes for the gift of healing; around ninety percent of the people in these fellowships have prayed for a sick person and have seen them healed.

These numbers are much higher than what we see in other places. The only difference is that, in house fellowships, we tend to make use of the gifts that God has given us much more often than those sitting in a traditional church setting. Those in house fellowships are using their gifts to make disciples through the authority of example, just like Jesus did. They are using the gifts God gave them to equip the saints to be able to serve, which, among other things, involves sharing Jesus and healing the sick. I have done a teaching called "Healing the sick – an hour is all it takes." It is a short lesson on what the Bible says about healing the sick, with a very practical side to it.

Many years ago, I was asked to teach a workshop at a Bible camp. I decided that my teaching would be called "Healing the sick – an hour is all it takes." It was a short lesson on what the Bible says about healing the sick, with a very practical side to it. I really wanted a fresh testimony and not just empty words when I said it only takes an hour to "learn" how to heal the sick. So the day before I was to teach, I contacted a new Christian who had been saved only one month. I asked him if he would be willing to pray for the sick, see them healed, and if I could have an hour of his time? He agreed. I looked at the clock and saw that it was 3:36 PM. I told him that we would stand in the same place, and by the time it was 4:36 PM, he would have shared the gospel of Jesus, prayed for a sick person, and seen that person healed.

We jumped into the car and drove to town. On the way, I gave him a short lesson on praying for the sick. When we arrived, I said: "Come, follow me." We walked around a bit, and, at some point, I started talking to some people on the street. The guy followed me and saw what I said and did. One woman had pain in her back, and I prayed for her. After this, I said to the new Christian: "Come with me. It is now your turn." We walked around while I assured him that he just had to do what he had seen me do. I caught sight of a young man and sensed that we should go to him. I told the new Christian what he should say. He put his hands on the young man and prayed. The man's knee was instantly healed, and both young men were very excited about what had happened.

Within that hour, four people had been healed, and we had shared the gospel with even more. The new Christian had prayed for two people, and I had prayed for two. He was extremely enthusiastic and went all around the Bible camp telling people what had just happened, even though I told him that he should not tell everyone. This reminds me of Jesus' disciples; they could not keep quiet about what they had experienced either.

> *And they called them and commanded them not to speak at all nor teach in the name of Jesus. But Peter and John answered and said to them, "Whether it is right in the sight of God to listen to you more than to God, you judge. For we cannot but speak the things which we have seen and heard." (Acts 4:18-20)*

This young Christian learned a lesson he will never forget. There is nothing as exciting as experiencing God working through you! Again: *we remember much more of what we do than of what we only hear.*

This is just one example of how we should teach today. If we start using these teaching methods again in our fellowships, people will grow like never before. Now, imagine for just a moment that we could see the whole five-fold ministry functioning in the same way. There would be no limit to what could happen. The fellowship would grow like never before, in a balanced way, where all gifts work together.

What that new Christian learned in just an hour many Christians cannot do after ten years in the church. They have heard that they should tell people about Jesus, and they know that they can pray for the sick, but do they do it? No! Often, they are not doing it because the step from sitting in the church pew to going out and doing it all by themselves in the world is simply too big. They are full of fear, and I cannot blame them. They actually need someone to equip them. They are missing the element of discipleship. You do not become a disciple by sitting, year in and year out, just listening to teachings. You become a disciple when someone takes you by the hand and says, "Come, follow me." It is about being together and sharing life. It is about being taught by more mature disciples with whom you spend time. A disciple is someone who makes others into disciples. As disciples, we should learn from those who are more mature how to live out the Christian life on a daily basis. Learn how to be a husband or wife, raise children, look after the house and home, give and reach out to each other, etc. This principle actually applies to all areas of life, not just to sharing Jesus and praying for the sick. We have to begin to build biblical fellowships, fellowships that make people into disciples, because that is what Jesus has commanded us to do.

Several things happened at the Bible camp that day. In addition to four people getting healed, the new Christian had a day to remember. There is nothing as wonderful as being used by God. It is something we need to experience over and over again in order to keep us burning and feeling alive. When the young man prayed for the last person who was healed in that hour, I let him do it all by himself. I went far away, for his sake, so that he would know the healing had nothing to do with me and that he was "trained" and could continue on his own without me being there. And so he did, even after I had driven away.

Some readers are bound to think this practice sounds robotic, and many will not like it that I say I teach people to heal because only God can heal. I agree. Only God can heal! The truth is that He has given this gift to the fellowship in order to guarantee that we Christians continue His work on the earth. It may seem weird to some that I did this only to have an illustration for what I was going to talk about the next day. The truth is that, even though it might seem that way, God was in on it. He has made His will clear once and for all:

"And heal the sick there, and say to them, 'The kingdom of God has come near to you.' " (Luke 10:9)

The proof of how much God had been involved in all of this came the very same evening. I went to a meeting where the worship leader suddenly asked if we could pray with her for her son, who was not living for God. His name was Jeppe. The whole fellowship began praying for him. When I heard his name, I thought: "Jeppe. We prayed for someone named Jeppe today." When the worship leader got down from the stage, I asked her if her son had a problem with his big toe. She looked at me, completely shocked, and said, "Yes!" I then said: "Well, he does not anymore!" I then told her how we had met him, how the newly saved Christian had prayed for him, and that her son had been healed. This all confirmed that my little "experiment" was actually an answer to the prayers of other people.

If we desire to see people grow and serve the Lord in their everyday lives, we have to use the gifts that God has given to the fellowship. Through the authority of example, Christians can learn in just an hour what many still do not dare to do after 10 or 15 years of sitting in the church. Do we want to use these gifts and return to working and training by example so that fear will disappear?

If we dare to put our culture behind us, forget what we usually do, and begin doing what Jesus and the first Christians did, we will see a fellowship rise where people are freely living as disciples of Jesus Christ in their everyday lives.

There are many different ministries and gifts in the fellowship. I'm not saying that everyone should do the same things I am doing. I am saying that I, like many others, have been given to the fellowship to equip other believers.

It is sobering to see a newly-saved young man experience more in one hour than many Christians who have sat in church for years. The way forward is for these gifts to be used in the right way again. The church is not being equipped by sitting and seeing an evangelist holding one campaign after another, or a prophet giving one prophecy after another. No, the five-fold ministry must equip believers so that everyone can get started, not only with using their gifts, but also teaching others to do the same. Further, we cannot help each other grow as Jesus' disciples by only meeting each other a couple of hours on a Sunday morning. If people are to learn to live a life of commitment to God and His Word, then we must spend time with them and train them through example.

May God raise up role models in our land so that the fellowship can grow as it should grow.

18

THE FIVE-FOLD MINISTRY

What would happen if a new Christian belonged to a fellowship where he followed other disciples on a daily basis and learned from their lives, as well as the five-fold ministry that God has placed in the church? He would grow at record speed, as it was in the first churches that were small, self-sufficient house fellowships. These self-sufficient house fellowships, though not independent, were connected to each other by the five-fold ministry. Those in the five-fold ministry are actually meant to be traveling ministries. New Christians mostly learned from the other disciples in the fellowship, but sometimes they were visited by traveling ministers who also contributed to their equipping.

This is what Paul said to the fellowship in Rome:

For I long to see you, that I may impart to you some spiritual gift, so that you may be established, that is, that I may be encouraged together with you by the mutual faith both of you and me. (Romans 1:11-12)

Paul visited different fellowships to give them gifts of the Spirit in order to strengthen them. The five-fold ministry was primarily made up of traveling ministries. The office of "pastor" did not mean a pastor of one particular fellowship, such as we have today. A pastor was someone who visited and traveled between different, self-sufficient fellowships, who came with a specific concern for the fellowship. He would pass this on to the believers there so they, in turn, would be better at showing concern for each other.

The small fellowships we see in the Bible were led by those the Bible calls "elders," or "overseers." These were also called "bishops." The problem is that, today, we come up with our own definitions for these words. If I say "pastor," you automatically think of a person who leads a church, meets in a building, and has church services every Sunday. This definition does not exist in the Bible.

There is no clear description in the Bible of the different ministries within the five-fold ministry. We only find more information about them in the history books. A lot of what we connect with these ministries today comes from our church culture.

I remember someone who came to me a few years ago saying that I definitely should not start a fellowship. The reason for it was that I was not a pastor but an evangelist, and evangelists were not meant to do that. Since I believed what he said, I struggled with it for a long time. One day I was in Copenhagen with seven people from seven different countries who worked with a ministry called "DAWN," which stands for "Disciple A Whole Nation." The main goal of DAWN is to mobilize the whole body of Christ and to equip 20,000 co-workers to train 2,000,000 churches so that together they can plant 20,000,000 other churches before 2020. When I met them, someone asked what my ministry was. At that point, I looked down to the ground and answered that I probably was an evangelist. Much to my surprise, he answered, "Fantastic! We have a great need for evangelists to start fellowships, since pastors are not really called for this."

His answer was a shock to me. At that point in time, I was feeling pretty down because people had just told me that I was rebellious for wanting to start a fellowship. The truth is that, in Denmark, we are living in a little bubble. We are doing things without questioning why and without questioning whether what we are doing is right. Further, if anyone is doing it differently, they are probably rebellious and should be put back in place; even though people outside our little bubble are actually doing things the very same way. House fellowships are actually the fastest growing church movement in the whole world. But many churches in Denmark do not realize this yet and do not see that they are fighting against the trend. What I am trying to say is that we should not focus so much on what ministry each person has. We should just do what is given to us and forget all about titles.

When I got saved more than fifteen years ago, I had just one thing on my heart, and that was to reach out to non-Christians. The Christians around me did not say anything at the time, but as my ministry grew, my focus and my heart changed. Today, I no longer see myself primarily as an evangelist but rather as an apostle, something which has been confirmed by many.

The whole issue of calling and ministry is something we grow into, and things change over time. You might have one ministry at a certain point in time and another a few years later. We too often stereotype each other too quickly. As I said before, we define the different ministries based on our church culture and not on what we read in the Bible. I will explain this to you with an example.

If I use the word "apostle," what would you think of? I believe that most of us would think of someone important, perhaps the highest position in the church today. If this is the case with you, you probably have a hard time with the fact that I see myself as an apostle. You might have thought: "How can he say such a thing? Who does he think he is?" This just shows you how we think. I wrote this to demonstrate that we define terms based mostly on our culture and not on what the Bible says. Further, it shows that we all suffer from peer pressure, and by doing so, we keep each other from excelling. But that subject is for another time.

When we read about the five-fold ministry in Ephesians, are they listed in order of importance, or do they indicate a certain hierarchy? If so, then the most important ministry is that of an apostle, then the prophet, then the evangelist, then the pastor, and finally, the teacher. But if they are in order of hierarchy why then is the ministry of the teacher number three in the list in the letter to the Corinthians? And what about the other ministries mentioned here? Where are they in the hierarchy?

And God has appointed these in the church: first apostles, second prophets, third teachers, after that miracles, then gifts of healings, helps, administrations, varieties of tongues. (1 Cor. 12:28)

Where did the evangelists and pastors go? Why have teachers suddenly been pushed up two places? The truth is that we should not get too caught up with the issue of importance or hierarchy. The bottom line is that we all are simply brothers and sisters.

What does Paul really have to say about apostles?

For I think that God has displayed us, the apostles, last, as men condemned to death; for we have been made a spectacle to the world, both to angels and to men. We are fools for Christ's sake, but you are wise in Christ! We are weak, but you are strong! You are distinguished, but we are dishonored! To the present hour we both hunger and thirst, and we are poorly clothed, and beaten, and homeless. And we labor, working with our own hands. Being reviled, we bless; being persecuted, we endure; being defamed, we entreat. We have been made as the filth of the world, the offscouring of all things until now. (1 Cor. 4:9-13)

This is the picture Paul gives of what it really means to be an apostle, a picture that does not exactly agree with the picture we have today. An apostle today is not one who is despised. Quite the opposite, he often is the cherry on the cake. The apostle is the one who is picked up in a big car and arrives in the middle of worship. At least, that is the way it is in some places. The word "apostle" actually means "sent out," but do you know where it comes from?

In Paul's time, a large part of the population consisted of slaves. One third of the population had slaves, and another third were slaves themselves. And many of the others were former slaves. A lord used his slaves for many different tasks, one of which was to deliver messages. Today, we use the post office and computers to send messages, but in those days it was the task of a slave to go out with a message from his master. In those days, going out with a message was not a safe task.

For this reason, a lord often sent soldiers with the slave messenger in order to ensure that the slave arrived with the message and got back safely. Sometimes there was no escort available, or it was simply too costly. In that case, the lord would send out the slave who was the least important, the one who would be missed the least if anything happened to him. The lord chose the most despised slave, and the word for this slave is "apostle."

I do realize that this is not what we think of when we hear the word "apostle," but it very much supports what Paul wrote about being an apostle. What I am not saying, however, is that an apostle has a lesser responsibility than the other ministers because they do not!!

> *… having been built on the foundation of the apostles and prophets, Jesus Christ Himself being the chief cornerstone.* (Eph. 2:20)

Here we read that it is primarily the apostles and the prophets who lay the foundation of the fellowship. They give direction to what God has planned to do, which naturally gives them a bigger responsibility. Also, teachers will be judged more strictly because of the responsibility they have—to lead no one astray.

> *My brethren, let not many of you become teachers, knowing that we shall receive a stricter judgment.* (James 3:1)

The different ministry offices have been given different responsibilities, and we need to recognize this, but having a bigger responsibility does not necessarily mean that we are above others. Remember that we are all brothers and sisters, and none of these ministries should rule over the rest of the Body. Furthermore, there is no hierarchy in the five-fold ministries; they are standing side by side. They are not to rule over people like we so often see today. These ministries are to serve and equip believers. They are there to lay a foundation so that those who believe have something on which to build.

When arriving at someone's house for a visit, one does not say, "Oh, what a lovely foundation this house has." The foundation is not even noticed. The only thing that is noticed is the house itself. It is the same with these ministries. They are there as a foundation, not to take all the honor.

According to the grace of God which was given to me, as a wise master builder I have laid the foundation, and another builds on it. But let each one take heed how he builds on it. (1 Cor. 3:10)

The purpose of these ministries is to serve and equip believers, so they, too, can serve. The goal is for all believers to be equipped for ministry, and this should be the focus of each fellowship. The five-fold ministries should not be doing the job for the saints but should be equipping the saints to do it themselves, for the Lord.

Therefore, be free and do what the Lord has called you to do!

19

LEADERSHIP

A big obstacle for fellowships today is how to function like the early church in the structure of leadership. In most places, this structure looks like a pyramid, with one leader at the top of the organization. If you look at the way the church was structured in the New Testament, you will see that it had a very flat structure.

This flat structure was something I had a hard time seeing in the beginning. I came from a fellowship with a pyramid structure, and I believed it was the only way to do things. Today, I can see that the Bible only talks about a flat structure, in both leadership and in the whole fellowship as well. The pyramid structure we find in most fellowships today is actually based on the Old Testament. We do not find it in the New Testament anymore because it is exactly what Jesus did away with.

Let's look at a few things Jesus said and did that go directly against much of what we see practiced today. In the gospel of John, we can read about Jesus washing his disciples' feet. He does this to teach them a lesson they will never forget—a lesson on leadership. We read:

So when He had washed their feet, taken His garments, and sat down again, He said to them, "Do you know what I have done to you? You call Me Teacher and Lord, and you say well, for so I am. If I then, your Lord and Teacher, have washed your feet, you also ought to wash one another's feet. For I have given you an example, that you should do as I have done to you. Most assuredly, I say to you, a servant is not greater than his master; nor is he who is sent greater than he who sent him. If you know these things, blessed are you if you do them." (John 13:12-17)

Why did Jesus wash the disciples' feet? The answer is, because they were dirty! In those days, people would lie down to eat in such a way that their neighbor's feet would be next to their head. Therefore, the feet were always washed before eating. In those days, one usually had slaves to do this job. They would wash the feet of their masters before their meal. Jesus washed the disciples' feet to demonstrate a point. He took the slaves' job and said that they were obliged to do the same. Later, He even came with this warning:

"But you, do not be called 'Rabbi'; for One is your Teacher, the Christ, and you are all brethren. Do not call anyone on earth your father; for One is your Father, He who is in heaven. And do not be called teachers; for One is your Teacher, the Christ. But he who is greatest among you shall be your servant. And whoever exalts himself will be humbled, and he who humbles himself will be exalted." (Matt. 23:8-12)

Should we wash each other's feet, as some are doing today? No. Jesus did not wash his disciples' feet to start a new religious tradition. Instead, we should understand that Jesus is saying we should serve one another. We are all brothers and sisters, just like He says here. The same goes for leaders. We should not start washing people's feet today because it is not a part of our culture. We do not recline at the table, and we do not have dusty, dirty feet. However, we should find ways to serve one another. For example, we could wash each other's cars if they are dirty.

Jesus came to serve, and He presented a structure that is different from what we see today. Jesus did not present a pyramid structure where He put a "man of God" at the top whom everyone else "serves." This method will surely fail because pride goes before a fall. No human is called to sit alone at the top of a pyramid.

The idea of a "man of God," as we see practiced in many places today, does not follow New Testament thinking either. If you want to find support for this idea in the Bible, you must, again, go back to the Old Testament. I am not saying that there should not be someone who leads. I am also not saying that there are not certain ministries in the fellowship that we should recognize and honor, but there needs to be a sound balance.

In Revelation 2, we read of a fellowship in Pergamum. Not everything that is said is very positive:

> *"Thus you also have those who hold the doctrine of the Nicolaitans, which thing I hate. 'Repent, or else I will come to you quickly and will fight against them with the sword of my mouth.' "* (Rev. 2:15-16)

At another place, we read that Jesus hates the teachings and deeds of the Nicolaitans. What is the teaching of the Nicolaitans? The word Nicolaitans comes from two words: "Nikos" and "Laos." It means "victory over the people" or "reign over the people." It is from the word "Laos" that we get the word "layman." So Jesus hates the teaching that certain people rule over laymen. The fact that we have leaders and pastors today who are reigning and making decisions over people is contrary to what we find in the Bible. This is a teaching that Jesus clearly hates. The idea that only priests, pastors, and leaders can baptize, share communion, share God's Word, etc., is something we do not find in the New Testament. According to Jesus, there is no such thing as a "layman" or a "professional." We are all brothers and sisters and have the same access to God because of Jesus' sacrifice. In other words, everyone has the same permission to hear from Him, baptize others, and so on. Even today, we need to do away with the teachings of the Nicolaitans, the idea that priests rank higher up in the hierarchy than laymen. This is plainly unbiblical, and Jesus hates it. Like I said, there clearly are ministries and leaders in the fellowship, but they have been put there to build the foundation and not to be the top of the man-made hierarchy. They are there to show the way and to go before, not to steer and decide.

I have experienced many times how church leaders put themselves in elevated positions over the people in the fellowship. These leaders may teach that you have to "obey your leader" in order to keep people in their places. Yet, they forget that, even though they are leaders, they are still first and foremost brothers and sisters. The people in these fellowships have access to God and can hear from Him in the same way as do the leaders.

Recently, a young woman came to me and asked me for advice. She had been involved in short term missions before and had a wonderful time. Now, once again, she began to sense Jesus calling her to pursue cross-cultural ministry. The leader of the fellowship she attended told her that she was not ready and that, "God would always talk to the leaders about something like that," so she should listen to them. I knew the girl well and knew that she was mature. Therefore, I could say that if God had said "go," she should go. The idea that God should always verify things through a leader is a lie. Some will surely see this as rebellion, but I strongly believe in this principle.

You might ask, "How can you say that when her leader had said something else?" I can say that because she is the one who will be held accountable for her own life and for what God has spoken to her. A leader can give advice and guidance but cannot decide over another person's life.

I can see that, in some churches, the leaders use fear to control their members. They come again and again with scary examples of people who have not obeyed their leaders and what happened as a result. They are saying indirectly, "This can happen to you, too, if you go against your leader." In response to this, I would like to say that I have only gotten to where I am today because I have not always obeyed my leaders. If I had obeyed my leaders, my ministry would have ended like I said in the beginning of the book. The question was whether I would obey my leader or God.

Many times, I have seen this Bible text being misused in order to control people:

> Obey those who rule over you, and be submissive, for they watch out for your souls, as those who must give account. Let them do so with joy and not with grief, for that would be unprofitable for you. (Heb. 13:17)

If you dig into the original text, this verse read something like this: "Listen to those who guide you and be convinced by them ..." It is about listening and being convinced by the Word, not about blindly following every command of a leader, despite what God has spoken to you.

When I see a Christian who is living in conscious sin, however, and he is not listening to his leader, I am also going to read this verse from the Bible to him. I would say that he should listen to his leader and be convinced by the Word of God. But if the leader is saying to a mature Christian: "You should not go away as a missionary," or "I believe that you should sell your car and give the money to me," I would say, "Don't listen to him because what they're saying is not biblical!"

Can you see how things can be misused when they are taken out of context? Imagine if I was a leader and went to visit some people from the fellowship. Do I then have the right to decide where their piano should be placed? And, if they do not listen, do I have the right to say: "I am your leader, and you must obey me?" No way! When I go before them and guide them from the Word, then I am surely their leader, but I do not have the right or the authority to decide over their lives. I can only guide them based on the truth of the Word, but they have the right to allow themselves to be convinced.

In the book, *Paul's Idea of Community*, Robert Banks shows how Paul used his authority. Paul never used his authority to dominate people or decide over them. He did not even decide over the fellowships that he had started himself. He guided them like a father and challenged them, but he never dominated over them or decided for them like we see people doing today. His relationship with the other apostles also shows that he was not placed under them in any way. For example, he was not afraid to correct the Apostle Peter when he made a mistake, although Peter had walked with Jesus. But he always challenged from the Word, which is the highest authority. As a leader, you are not to lord over people; we are co-workers like Paul says here:

Not that we have dominion over your faith, but are fellow workers for your joy; for by faith you stand. (2 Cor. 1:24)

The author of Hebrews clearly describes what leadership is about:

Remember those who rule over you, who have spoken the word of God to you, whose faith follow, considering the outcome of their conduct. Jesus Christ is the same yesterday, today, and forever. (Heb. 13:7-8)

Peter has this to say to the leaders in the fellowship:

Shepherd the flock of God which is among you, serving as overseers, not by compulsion but willingly, not for dishonest gain but eagerly; nor as being lords over those entrusted to you, but being examples to the flock; and when the Chief Shepherd appears, you will receive the crown of glory that does not fade away. (1 Peter 5:2-4)

Leadership is not about making yourself the ruler over another person's life. Leadership is about being an example. Being a leader is not about standing over others; it is about going before others. A leader goes ahead and lets the others decide for themselves whether they want to follow or not. When those whom God has placed as leaders in the fellowship understand this, they will experience a greater freedom as well.

It is freeing to realize that we are not responsible for other people's lives. As a leader, one only needs to go first and show the way. After that, it is up to the others to follow.

I have seen an almost demonic teaching in some free churches today that I have come to call "spiritual covering." It starts by saying that you need to have a spiritual leader over you. Otherwise, you are not protected. This teaching also points out that having a spiritual leader is necessary to experiencing God's anointing on your life. The leaders teaching these things also have someone they call their leader or spiritual authority, but those people are usually abroad, or at least very far away. It is much easier to "obey" someone very far away than to obey your brothers nearby.

For a long time, this issue was a great challenge for me. I came from a free church where this way of thinking had been deeply rooted in me. It was difficult for me because, so many times, I had been in situations where a choice was put in front of me: Should I obey my leaders, or should I follow what I experienced God saying? It was at one of these precise moments that I received a visit from Steve Hill for the first time, and he just happened to teach precisely on this point. His teaching really helped to set me free in this area.

Not everyone can understand what I'm talking about here, but many unfortunately do. Steve Hill showed me what a true Christian leader and father in the faith actually is. For the first time, with all of my heart, I could recognize a true leader. I suddenly realized that the reason I had such a problem with this was not because of me or because I was rebellious. Rather, it was because I was in a system full of control that did not build upon the structure we read about in the New Testament. Further, this is the type of control that results in only a few coming out into the calling and ministry the Lord has given them. This incorrect teaching on "spiritual covering" keeps people imprisoned in a system where they can not go any further.

Obedience is important. The Bible talks a lot about obedience and submission. It even talks about submitting to one another:

... submitting to one another in the fear of God. (Eph. 5:21)

So we really should submit to each other, not to a leader who lives very far away and does not even know how we live day by day. We have need for a flat structure that can set people free, free to hear God for themselves and take responsibility for their own lives. The structure that many churches have today limits the growth and functionality of too many members of the body.

We are all brothers and sisters, and the Head of the fellowship is not the pastor nor the leader; it's Jesus Christ. He wants to talk to us all. When the first fellowships gathered together, they all sought Jesus and let Him talk through them. We are not talking about creating anarchy or chaos, which is what many fear. There is a Lord who leads the church, and He is Jesus Christ.

I know very well that, in many fellowships, we are not going to be able to have this flat structure without it going completely crazy. The reason for this is that many members in the fellowship have not really "come through." They are still living with themselves as lord and following their own lusts instead of God's will. But if you have given yourself totally to Christ, and you only have God's will and His eyes, then this idea of a flat structure is not a problem—quite the opposite!

There are, of course, leaders in God's fellowship, but they are not called to dominate people and make decisions for them. When you stand as a leader, you are still brother to the others in the fellowship. You stand side by side and not over anyone. You go before so that others can follow.

I believe it is so important that we start to see and function according to a godly structure again. I am convinced that God is going to raise up good, sound leaders who, as spiritual fathers, can lay down a good foundation for the fellowship to grow in Christ.

20

THE HOLY SPIRIT

I clearly remember a time in my life when I was unbelievably pressured. I was in a fellowship, and I had responsibility for people in that fellowship. I believed that the responsibility for their lives rested on me because I was their pastor. If they were having a difficult time, it was probably because I was a bad leader. If they were having good times, then it was because I was a good leader.

Luckily, God showed me how wrong this idea was. He set me free and taught me a couple of lessons that I will never forget. Before I received these lessons, I could not even manage leading our little fellowship with only a few new believers. After the lessons, it would not have been a problem if I had a million new believers to lead. The difference is that God taught me two very important points.

The first is in regard to how we see leadership. I am clearly a leader, but I cannot and will not steer or control people's lives. I can only lay a foundation, and then it is up to each person to build on it.

Jesus was the best Leader in history, despite Judas' choosing to betray Him. This means that we probably will not escape experiencing this either. I have learned that being a leader is not so important and that I should learn to let go. Even though Jesus was the best Leader who ever existed, He still said to His disciples that it was better for them if He left them.

"Nevertheless I tell you the truth. It is to your advantage that I go away; for if I do not go away, the Helper will not come to you; but if I depart, I will send Him to you." (John 16:7)

If it was better for them that Jesus, the best Leader ever, left them, how can we then believe that we are irreplaceable? Maybe it is because we do not have enough trust in the Holy Spirit. This leads to another important point I learned.

One day, my friend, Steve Hill, asked me a question: "What is the Holy Spirit's job?" I answered that it was to remind us what Jesus had said, as well as convict us of our sin, of righteousness, and of judgment. He then asked me how good the Holy Spirit was at doing this. I did not know what I was supposed to answer other than that He was really good at it. He then asked me how I thought we should divide the work between us, whether I was responsible for forty percent and the Holy Spirit for sixty percent, or the opposite.

This really got me thinking. There is no one better at doing all of these things than the Holy Spirit. It was for this reason exactly that Jesus could say it was better that He left. That day, I learned a little bit more about the Holy Spirit, and it really set me free in my role as a leader.

I do understand why many leaders and pastors suffer from stress in the church system we have today. Everything depends on them! If the church grows, the pastor is good. If it does not grow and if people have problems, then it is also the pastor's fault. It is impossible to live that way long term, and it was never God's plan in the first place. We need to go back to the flat structure where Jesus is the Head of the fellowship and the Holy Spirit is allowed to work in all of us.

I can bear witness to many great things that happened when I let go. People were saved and grew like never before. All of us understood that I did not have responsibility for them, which made them take responsibility for themselves. They understood that it was the Holy Spirit's task to teach them and remind them about sin, etc., which made them listen to the Holy Spirit more. As a result, they were changed. Now, the number of people is not a problem anymore because the Holy Spirit is big enough for all people and all of their needs.

Let's read something from the book of 1 John that is unbelievably radical, something I know many today have a hard time understanding:

But the anointing which you have received from Him abides in you, and you do not need that anyone teach you; but as the same anointing teaches you concerning all things, and is true, and is not a lie, and just as it has taught you, you will abide in Him. (1 John 2:27)

I am not saying that all teaching is unnecessary. When we read this verse, we need to realize there is something we have forgotten. Think! It actually says that we do not need anyone else to teach us because we now have the Holy Spirit! The same thing is explained in a different way in the letter to the Hebrews when it talks about the new covenant:

"For this is the covenant that I will make with the house of Israel after those days, says the Lord: I will put My laws in their mind and write them on their hearts; and I will be their God, and they shall be My people. None of them shall teach his neighbor, and none his brother, saying, 'Know the Lord,' for all shall know Me, from the least of them to the greatest of them. For I will be merciful to their unrighteousness, and their sins and their lawless deeds I will remember no more." (Heb. 8:10-12)

We are reading here about a whole new covenant. Today, we all have access to God through Jesus Christ. We can all know God and be led by Him. Like we read here, He sent His Holy Spirit to guide us and to show us Who He is.

Why do we not have more confidence in this? Why do we still believe that people need a middleman—a pastor—to know God's will and to live the life to which God has called us? Maybe it is because we have churches where many are not even saved. Many have gotten a touch from God and prayed to Him and are now coming to church faithfully, but they have never really "come through" to salvation, and now we are trying to organize "babysitters" for them.

Since they have not really "come through," we are not going to see the Holy Spirit doing the same in them as we see Him doing in others who really are saved. Instead, we pretend to be the Holy Spirit ourselves. We try to raise them to live like true disciples of Jesus, but we are not doing them any favors. Rather, the opposite. We should be showing them that they have not really come through yet. When they turn completely and experience the new birth like Jesus talks about, then the Holy Spirit will take over and will work in them. They will then be led by the Spirit instead of the flesh, like the letter to the Romans talks about. This is a sign of a true Christian.

Again, it is about preaching the gospel as radically and as straightforward as we can without candy coating it. Then we will see people turning around and being saved. The Holy Spirit will then come and work in them exactly like we read in the Bible.

It is not God who has changed, but we have changed the gospel in such a way that the church is often full of people who are not really saved. Nowadays, I see pastors spend hours, weeks, and even months giving advice and helping people within their churches. Yet, many of these issues would be resolved automatically if people would simply repent and get saved. We should use the time to lead them to salvation instead of being their advisors on all kinds of issues and trying to do the Holy Spirit's work.

"And when He has come, He will convict the world of sin, and of righteousness, and of judgment: ... He will guide you into all truth ..." (John 16:8, 13)

When I was saved on April 5, 1995, I came from a world totally outside the church. I had experienced sin just like many young people in the world have today. However, from the day I was saved, the Holy Spirit began a work in my life, just as we read about in the Bible. The Holy Spirit taught me through the Word, and I began turning away from my old life. In all of my years as a Christian, I still have not experienced the need for someone to check up on me. No one has ever reminded me that I do not get to live in sin anymore. No one has told me that I should remember to read my Bible, or that I should remember to come to meetings. No, none of that was necessary because I had really been saved. The Holy Spirit would show me what needed to change and how I should live. The Holy Spirit was the one teaching me, just like we read earlier. That is why He is here.

I see the same thing happening today when others turn to Him completely. When this happens, we do not need someone to tell them all these things because this is something the Holy Spirit does. In the beginning, when I was first saved, there were times when sin or my old friends would draw me in, but I simply could not let go of God. I was like one of the disciples when he answered Jesus after many had left Him:

> *Then Jesus said to the twelve, "Do you also want to go away?" But Simon Peter answered Him, "Lord, to whom shall we go? You have the words of eternal life. Also we have come to believe and know that You are the Christ, the Son of the living God."* (John 6:67-69)

In Acts, chapter eight, we read about Philip baptizing the Ethiopian eunuch. After the eunuch was baptized, God took Philip to another place, and the eunuch was left alone. He was completely new in the faith, and the only thing he had was the text from the Old Testament. However, he was not all alone. He had the Holy Spirit! God had complete control over the eunuch and took Philip away. God had given the eunuch a Helper for life, the Holy Spirit.

If we begin preaching the gospel as it was intended by Jesus and let the Holy Spirit come, then He is going to convince people of their sin so they truly repent. He is going to teach them and continue the good work in them that He has begun (Philippians 1:6).

The first fellowships saw how the Holy Spirit was present among people. The Holy Spirit was a big part of their lives, and they could say: *"For it seemed good to the Holy Spirit, and to us ..."* (Acts 15:28). It was not just the people in the fellowship who made decisions. No, they let the Holy Spirit take His rightful place in the fellowship.

This is another reason the fellowship at that time is so very different from what we see in many places today. The fellowship could function as a flat structure, without any chaos and without people causing uproar, because Jesus' presence was so powerfully represented through the Holy Spirit. No one but Jesus was the Head of the fellowship, and it was clear to everyone.

Today, the church is filled with "fleshly" people, and this is the main reason why the current New Testament church structure that we see in many places simply will not work. As a result of this fleshliness, we have been led to develop the structures that we have today. It is simply a replacement for the real thing. The same goes for the style in which we conduct our meetings today. Just think about all of the energy we spend creating the feeling that the Holy Spirit is close. We do not need a dark room with candlelight or emotional music or anything else if the Holy Spirit is truly there. Instead, this is an indication that He is not present the way we see it in the Bible.

We can not allow ourselves to be tricked into believing this new structure and style (the pretty packaging) is the right way to do things. If we build churches with "fleshly" people, they are only going to hold out until the day we truly stand face to face with God.

"But if we take all of this away, everyone will stop coming!" many will say. Yes, but maybe this is an even bigger reason to lay aside these things because then we will see what has truly been built by God. Remember, it is Jesus who will build His church, not us! We are but "living stones," and Jesus will build His church the way He wants it!

Today, we see what many are calling the twenty-eighty rule. It comes from the idea that, in a normal traditional fellowship, twenty percent of the people do all the work, while the other eighty percent only come and enjoy the meetings. It was like this in China, too, right before the communists came and took power in 1949. When they came to power, it brought great persecution to the saints, and all the missionaries were thrown out of the country. This meant that all of the churches closed, and the eighty percent of those who had earlier gone to church "fell away." After the persecution, only about twenty percent were left—the twenty percent who had been doing all the work. The truth is, the eighty percent had not really "fallen away" because they had never really been a part. If they had truly "come through" to salvation, they would never have fallen away but would have been willing to pay the price. It so happened that because the fellowship now only consisted of a few true disciples who were willing to pay the price, they could give themselves totally to the Lord. This was the start of the great revival that we are still seeing in China today, where millions are turning to God. However, all of this is taking place through small house groups, so no one really knows exactly how many millions of new believers we are talking about.

The Holy Spirit is the same today! Today, unfortunately, He has been replaced by a system that keeps people trapped in a false faith. A system and hierarchy can never take the place of the Holy Spirit in a person's life. A system only creates a false picture of what the truth actually looks like. Hierarchy gives a false idea of everything being in order. The reality is that many are living in rebellion against God. Systems can get us to believe that people have "come through" when they really have not. A hierarchy can be a secret comfort zone for proud people who actually love to rule over people.

Other tasks of the Holy Spirit are to remind us of Jesus' words and to guide us into the truth.

"But the Helper, the Holy Spirit, whom the Father will send in My name, He will teach you all things, and bring to your remembrance all things that I said to you." (John 14:26)

"However, when He, the Spirit of truth, has come, He will guide you into all truth; for He will not speak on His own authority, but whatever He hears He will speak; and He will tell you things to come." (John 16:13)

I could continue with a long list of all the tasks and functions of the Holy Spirit, such as being a Helper, Comforter, Witness, and One who gives us power, etc. We have heard that it is very important to follow up on people. The truth is that, in the Bible, we do not see any following up the way we do it today. Today, we hear that following up is a necessity because newly saved people are like newborn babies. We all know that newborn babies cannot survive without their parents! Babies need their parents! And this logic is applied to newly born Christians as well—without spiritual parents, they will die.

It is true that newborn babies need their parents. It is also true that spiritually newborn people need parents, too. However, we forget that we are not the ones who gave birth to them. God has given birth to them, and He will certainly take care of them! He is their Father and has not left them fatherless. He has given them the Holy Spirit.

I'm not saying that we should just let people go or that I'm against all forms of checking up on people. We should be making people into disciples, as you have already read. There is a big difference, however, between letting people follow us and using our time to follow up on them. Jesus said, "Come, follow me," while He continued onward. If people have received the "inner witness," that they are truly born again, then they are automatically going to have "outer signs" as well. For example, these people will look for Christian fellowship. These are the people to whom we can say, "Come and follow me." We can go on before them without needing to look back all the time to check whether they are still with us. We need to remember how important it is that there is someone going before them. It is impossible to follow a car that is standing still. A car needs to be moving before anyone can follow it.

We should, of course, help and support one another, but it is not Jesus' task to follow up on us. It is our task to keep following Him.

So, yes, I do think that we can easily take all the outer things away and have a flat structure without people falling away, as long as they have really "come through" and have the Holy Spirit living inside them. Those who come to a fellowship with a flat structure, for the right reason, will grow and blossom in faith. There will be freedom and space for each individual to follow God and to do exactly what He has placed in the heart of each individual.

21
LOTS OF NEW CHURCHES

We have looked at the early church and compared it to the church of today. We have looked at how important it is to have the right structure. We have looked at the call that was given to all of us to make disciples and that this primarily happens through example. We have looked a little at the five-fold ministry and the importance of the work of the Holy Spirit. Now, we will look at another reason small house groups are important.

Small house fellowships are much easier and quicker to start than traditional free churches. When you start a traditional fellowship, you often need a facility and many hands helping you. All you need to start a house fellowship is an open home.

DAWN (Disciple A Whole Nation) works with the strategy of planting new fellowships. DAWN says that the optimal way to accomplish the Great Commission is to start one new fellowship for every 500 to 1,000 inhabitants because this is the best way to effectively reach people. DAWN came up with these numbers by looking at how big the sphere of influence of a medium to large fellowship is and then projecting this number on an entire population in order to determine how many fellowships are needed to reach an entire nation, which is what Jesus tells us to do in the Great Commission.

Based on this vision, Denmark, for example, needs many new fellowships. According to DAWN, a Danish city with 30,000 inhabitants should have 30 to 45 fellowships. Today, a city of this size has maybe one Pentecostal Church, one Free Church, maybe a Missionary Church, a Baptist Church, and some State Churches. We could say that, on average, a city of this size has a maximum of 5 to 6 living fellowships. According to the DAWN vision, there are still between 25 and 40 fellowships missing in order to accomplish the mission Jesus has given us.

> *And Jesus came and spoke to them, saying, "All authority has been given to Me in heaven and on earth. Go therefore and make disciples of all the nations, baptizing them in the name of the Father and of the Son and of the Holy Spirit, teaching them to observe all things that I have commanded you; and lo, I am with you always, even to the end of the age." Amen.* (Matt. 28:18-20)

Jesus commanded us to make disciples of all nations. He did not command us to only make disciples of a few people from every nation but *entire* nations. When we truly understand what Jesus has commanded us to do, we will start to have an entirely different idea about the true mission of the church than what most of us have today.

If Jesus had said that the goal is to make a few people from every nation into His disciples, then it would be logical for a church to have a vision to grow to 300 members. It would also be okay for the church to start a new fellowship every ten years. However, a church with 300 members that starts a new fellowship every ten years will never be able to accomplish the mission that Jesus has actually given us.

When we truly understand what Jesus is saying here, we will begin to realize that many today are actually aiming in the wrong direction and are missing the target. When we understand that Jesus was actually talking about discipling the entire nation, we are going to be forced to work very differently than how we are working today. For example, our goal will be to send people out who can start new fellowships as "soon" as possible. The "war" between fellowships for members will end, and we will be able to work together in order to reach our common goal. Denmark needs a lot of new fellowships if that is the best way to make the Danish nation into disciples of Jesus. This applies to all nations.

All the numbers show that a fellowship grows the most within the first two years after it is planted. Afterward, growth decreases and often even stops after the fellowship reaches a certain size. This corresponds with my own experience. When we started a new fellowship, other pastors in the city said the reason we were growing so much, compared to them, was because we were new, and that we should expect it to change after a few years. The logical question to ask, then, is this: *If this is true, why don't we start sending out people to start more new fellowships instead of trying to gather more people into the same place for many years?*

The truth is that new fellowships do tend to grow much more than old ones. There may be many reasons for this, but one of the reasons is surely that new fellowships are on God's heart.

I recently heard about a church in Australia that had not grown for many years. One day, a division took place that split the church into four smaller fellowships. At first, it seemed like something terrible had happened, but, in the end, it was only Satan who lost. What happened is that, suddenly, all four "new" fellowships started to grow again. After two years, all four fellowships were just as big as the original fellowship before the division. This is really interesting, and the same thing has happened in many other places.

Many of those who work with church statistics say that division can sometimes actually be God's way to move forward. They refer to the fact that the first Christians' mission was to go out and preach the gospel, but they did not do it. So God raised up a man called Saul. He persecuted the church so that it spread out, and wherever they went, there was great growth. I neither suggest nor hope that this would be necessary because division is always painful, and it often comes with much hardship.

According to Operation World (www.operationworld.org), there are a total of 200,000 cities in Europe without a single living fellowship; 200,000 cities, all of which need fellowships. This is on God's heart. The problem is simply that the laborers are often few, especially because they are so busy with church activities and the maintenance of their church buildings.

If a fellowship has not grown in many years, is it not about time to make some changes? One of the things that we could do is send people out to start new gatherings. Something is sure to happen.

We went through a transition in a fellowship that had fifty adult members. My wife and I left the fellowship to start our own. Suddenly, there were two fellowships, with forty-eight adults in one and two adults in the other. After some time, we had grown with about ten new Christians, which was more than the bigger fellowship had grown, but let's say, for example, that our old fellowship had also grown with ten new Christians. What would that tell us? Exactly what all the statistics show, that bigger fellowships do not necessarily mean bigger growth.

Imagine a fellowship with forty-eight members who are all doing the same things we are doing. They go out and start their own fellowship. We are not talking about making a big fellowship with a building, hundreds of members, worship groups, membership, rules, and services every Sunday. We are talking about a small home gathering with the goal of reaching at least ten people with the gospel within the first two years. Remember, this is surely possible, since new fellowships grow the most in the beginning.

I realize this might seem unrealistic for most Christians. They have been going to church for many years without seeing any growth. Now, they are supposed to think they can suddenly reach ten people in only two years. We need to understand, however, that when we go out on God's Word, He is going to bless it. In the book of Acts, we read that the growth came because God was adding to the fellowship daily. He is going to do the same today, if we are obedient. This type of growth is not impossible if you get the right teaching and the right practical help. In other countries, we see this happening again and again.

Let's say that these forty-eight members went out four by four so that they would not have to start alone. Instead of starting twenty-four new small house groups, they start twelve. Let's say that these twelve small house groups were able to grow by only half of what we had hoped. This would still mean that these twelve new fellowships would reach sixty new people for Jesus in the first two years.

Where do we find such growth? We do not find it anywhere that I know of. Imagine that each one of these twelve small groups decides to organize one event per year with an outward focus. This is not impossible since we are talking about only one a year. This would mean that the city is going to experience a total of twelve events each year.

What fellowship has the potential to organize twelve such events each year? The truth is that small fellowships are a really good idea because it means that we can reach out to many more non-Christians. Many small fellowships together have a bigger potential for growth than a few big fellowships.

What can we learn from this? We can learn that instead of gathering people in a church Sunday after Sunday without doing anything, we should use that time to make them into disciples so that they can quickly "leave home" and start their own fellowship. They do the same as a natural family: the children leave home and start their own families. After Jesus trained His disciples for a short time, He sent them out with these words:

> "But whatever house you enter, first say, 'Peace to this house.' And if a son of peace is there, your peace will rest on it; if not, it will return to you. And remain in the same house, eating and drinking such things as they give, for the laborer is worthy of his wages. Do not go from house to house. Whatever city you enter, and they receive you, eat such things as are set before you. And heal the sick there, and say to them, 'The kingdom of God has come near to you.'" (Luke 10:5-9)

Jesus laid the foundation for disciple making for the first Christians when they were sent out. It is about finding a "son/man of peace" and beginning a fellowship in that person's home. This is how they started! A man of peace is a person whom God has already called. He or she is someone who is ready to repent so that he and his household may be blessed. In Acts 16, we read what Paul and Silas experienced. The prison guard and his whole household were saved, and one more fellowship was born. This is how Peter started the new fellowship in Cornelius' home, too.

It can take many years to start a traditional fellowship today, but it can take just one day to start a house fellowship. The only thing that is needed is a man of peace. You begin to meet in his or her home, start inviting friends, and see how it grows. It is in this way that thousands of fellowships around the world are being started today. It does not need to be so hard, not even where you are.

Today, it seems like many people are stuck in the system, and pastors have a hard time sending people out. We do not see many new fellowships starting in Denmark. Instead, we see more and more fellowships joining together and getting bigger and bigger, but this, unfortunately, only results in more and more passive Christians who are not being made into disciples. All of the statistics show that when two fellowships join together, they will still be the same size after a few years as they were before they joined together. Joining two churches does not necessarily produce growth, only bigger numbers.

I personally know of several fellowships that have joined together, and the result was the same. After a few years, there were just as many gathering together as there were before they joined together. The only difference was that they had one less fellowship in town reaching out to people. That is why this is a bad idea. Of course, there are some exceptions, and it is these few success stories that we hear about. My advice is, however: listen to the statistics and learn from them!

When we started various fellowships, we experienced growth, mostly in the beginning. After a time, the growth came to a halt, just like the other pastors and the statistics said. There is something that happens in a fellowship when it grows to between 30 to 50 people. When the pastors told us that this would happen, we thought: "No, it will not go that way for us. We are going to continue in growth until we are many." But they were right. We did not know why it was like that or how we could have avoided it back then, but we do now.

Over the last few years, we have learned what we can do in order to continue to grow. What we must do is keep starting new fellowships all the time, everywhere. If it does not work, just close it down again. A fellowship closing is not necessarily a bad thing. It is not a defeat when people simply start meeting someplace else. We have started fellowships that have closed down again. This has made people spread to other places where they have seen growth. We should not be so afraid of this. It is not about gathering people in a certain place or fellowship. It is about sending people out. Instead of being one big fellowship, we can start fellowships ourselves, or help others start one of many small parts of the one fellowship of Christ.

People who work with this concept often split up into small fellowships when they become "too many." We also tried this, but it did not work for us. Splitting a fellowship can be difficult because good relationships are often split up. Instead of splitting, it is easier to avoid having too many in one place by building up new fellowships. In the other fellowship we had, for example, we saw a family in a neighboring town who got saved. When the family started coming to us in our living room, we had too many people. Instead of them coming to us, we should have sent out some people to help them start up in their own home. Unfortunately, we did not realize this back then because we were too busy trying to grow as much as possible. If we had done so, there would have been two fellowships instead of one, and we still could have met together every other week or once a month to praise God.

I am convinced that this is exactly what God wants to see happen. We are going to see many more self-sufficient fellowships around in different towns. These fellowships can come together every other week or once a month and be together to have a party and praise God. In this way, we can be small, self-sufficient fellowships and, at the same time, have big gatherings, which are also important.

This is, without a doubt, the way forward for the church in Denmark, as well as in other countries. In the last few years, we have actually baptized over one hundred people in different groups that we have helped to start up or through the relationships that we have built. I do not know of any other fellowship that has seen the same growth through so few people. The reason for this growth is that "church" and missions are not restricted to a specific place or a few people. It spreads like ripples in the water. New believers start fellowships in their homes and lead other families and friends to faith in Jesus Christ. It is those new believers who are baptizing the newer believers because they have led them to salvation. This can truly turn into a revolution that cannot be stopped, a revolution that spreads everywhere. We must start making disciples again as Jesus has commanded us.

I do not want to call the growth that we have experienced in the new fellowships "an awakening." However, even the small things we experience God doing today can become something really big if they continue to grow.

The last few times we have started up a new fellowship, around ten new people have been saved within two years, which in itself does not sound like a lot. In terms of growth, this means a growth of several hundred percentage points. Imagine a fellowship of fifty people that grows with only 100 percent per year! After one year, it would have 100 people, the year after 200, then 400, 800, 1600, 3200, etc. In fifteen years, this fellowship alone would have 1.6 million members and would be the world's biggest fellowship. The biggest church growth in the world right now is probably in China where the fellowship consists of small, self-sufficient gatherings. This probably explains why the growth is so significant. These new Christians were also discipled to follow Jesus and are growing fast because these small groups are the optimal environment for discipleship and personal growth.

Most of the churches in Denmark with 200 to 300 members actually have a very small percentage of growth. It could be that they are actually growing, but the percentage of growth is very low compared to their total size. The road forward must be to start many new small fellowships.

When we talk about fellowships today, we have a tendency to listen to some of the pastors in the United States who have started churches that grew to 10,000 members in only fifteen to twenty years.

This is excellent, of course, but the fact is that their growth in percentage points is actually not that big, especially when you count only new Christians. A big part of the growth of these churches is due to new members coming from other fellowships. The growth they have is still excellent but actually cannot come close to what we see in many other places around the world. In China, for example, we are seeing a completely different kind of growth. There, we are talking about small fellowships that are growing with several hundred thousand in the same fifteen to twenty years and where the growth rate increases over time. Of necessity, we just do not hear so much about it.

Imagine that we had 1,000 Christians in Denmark who would start 500 small fellowships all around Denmark. If they had the growth that we had, these 500 new fellowships would make 5,000 new Christians in just two years. Wow, that would be big.

Think what would happen if they made these 5,000 new believers into disciples so that they could do the same. In a few years, there would be 50,000 new Christians. If this would continue, then in fifteen to twenty years there would be 5,000,000 new Christians in Denmark. The only appropriate term for this is an awakening! (The population is approximately 5.6 million in Denmark at this writing.)

But what if our hypothetical experiment was not entirely realistic? Let's say we only see ten percent of the estimated growth. A tenth would still mean many hundreds of thousands of new Christians in a few years. Instead of waiting for something really big to happen, we can start with doing the small, simple things like so many others are doing. Start by doing what the Bible asks us to do!

22
SIMPLE GATHERINGS

Throughout this book, I have purposely used the term "house fellowship," but these words do not really express what I mean. The reason for this is that we see many house fellowships today that resemble traditional churches. They have a leader who is almost always the one who speaks, and they have a set program. Baptism is something the leader is responsible for. In other words, they are a small version of a traditional fellowship, and their church building is a home instead of a public building.

I know that many people have the same idea of house fellowships because they look like this in many places. Personally, if I had to choose between such a house fellowship and a traditional free church, I would probably choose the traditional (Free) church. It is *not* just about meeting in a home instead of in a church building. It is about everything else we have read about in this book. It is about making people into disciples of Jesus and, thus, obeying His commandment; for that, you do not even need to meet in a house. You could meet in a café on the beach, or any other place—yes, even in a church building. This sometimes requires a little extra effort, however, because many have the tendency to become so remarkably religious when they step into a church building. For this reason, I would like to try to avoid the word "fellowship," if I can, because, like the word "church," it tends to create a lot of expectations related to church culture. It is hard to avoid this word completely, however, since you would have a hard time knowing what it is we are talking about otherwise. Personally, I think the term "simple gatherings" better describes what God wants to initiate. It is about gathering with one other and with God. It is about the fact that we are disciples of Jesus, and we are to make others into disciples of Jesus, disciples who obey our Lord in word and in deed. It is about doing that as simply as possible, so that it is easy to multiply and expand. We must lay aside the church culture that is stopping us from building the church God wants us to be. Laying aside the church culture might be easier if we did not use the terms "church," "fellowship," or even "gatherings" at all.

If I were to ask someone from a traditional church whether they have the desire to start a fellowship or not, most of them would say, "No, thanks. I'll pass." Their idea of what planting a fellowship involves scares them. They have seen some of the problems that come with being the leader of a traditional fellowship. Think about all the money that is needed, the rules, the planning, the church politics, etc. It takes a lot of effort to start a traditional fellowship, and it is probably for this reason that we seldom see new fellowships being planted today. That is also the reason why more and more fellowships are actually missing a pastor.

I did not want to be pastor in a fellowship anywhere. Today, however, it would not be a problem if I were to start a new fellowship everyday, if God let it happen. It does not need to be as complicated as we tend to make it. You do not need rules, a website, a program, etc. You do not need to carry all of the responsibility alone. When in a simple gathering with a flat structure, everyone works together to feed the flock, and everyone helps out. In that case, the only thing that is really needed is for you to begin meeting up with some people and, together, focus on how we can all be disciples who obey what Jesus has commanded us. You can, for example, start with eating together and sharing Jesus with each other.

When you have friends visiting and are talking about Jesus, does one of you lead the evening? Have you set up a program for what should happen? No, not at all! Why make such a huge deal out of it when it is just as much church as a regular church meeting on Sunday? Jesus explains the only criteria that is necessary:

"For where two or three are gathered together in My name, I am there in the midst of them." (Matt. 18:20)

Invite people to your home to eat! Eat together and remember Jesus in sharing communion together! After you have eaten, everyone can share a bit about what they have experienced during the last few days. After that, you can pray together and seek God to hear what He wants to say to you. One or more can share something from the Bible, and you can talk about it. That is just an example of how things could be done. Just make sure that these things do not occur in the same way every time you meet because it can easily become a ritual again.

The truth is that most people have already done this with their friends and relatives, but they just have not thought of it as church. They simply had a nice, enjoyable evening, and everyone got a lot out of it. Yes, often, even more than they would get out of a "normal" church service. However, we do not think of it as "real church." Because of that, we do not practice it on a regular basis and do not give it much priority either.

But why is it this way? Why not continue meeting like this and sometimes invite non-Christians to your home instead of to church? If we do so, we will see growth! Why make it so complicated?

"Yeah, well, we need a pastor, of course, in order to start a fellowship." No, you do not! Where does it say so in the Bible? In the first fellowships, you found a man of peace and stayed with him. You met at his home and did the things we read about. You ate together, shared communion and life together. You prayed together and shared the Word. You were together with Christ. You listened to what Jesus wanted to say to you and then did it. The new disciples asked questions and learned from those who were more mature. You did not concentrate on who should be an elder or pastor because you were all together as a family. After some time, it would naturally become apparent to all who was an elder or host in the gathering—the one who went forward and held everything together. But that person did not control everything. You would lay hands on that person and appoint him an elder.

To appoint an elder was not like today where one delegates authority to a certain person. In the first fellowships it was rather a confirmation of the gift and calling that was already clear to everyone in the fellowship. This was not something they did on the first day of meeting together. It would happen after a while, when it became clear to everyone who the elder was. We read about what Paul said to Titus:

> For this reason I left you in Crete, that you should set in order the things that are lacking, and appoint elders in every city as I commanded you. (Titus 1:5)

These "appointed elders" were well known by the others in the fellowships, and, in this way, they could start serving the independent fellowships. It is about keeping things as simple as we see it in the Bible. You do not need membership, rules, programs, buildings, websites, and all that. Concerning finances, you simply give what you feel you should give. You can give to help each other, to spread the gospel, and to the traveling ministries that come to visit.

The first fellowships did not have any name either. This is what Paul wrote when he was thinking about a certain fellowship:

> "Greet the brethren who are in Laodicea, and Nymphas and the church that is in her house." (Col. 4:15)

(Notice that women could serve in the first fellowships, too, and I am not talking about serving food.)

So "fellowship in X's house or apartment" or "gathering in X's home" is good enough. Of course, it comes naturally to have a name, but again, keep it simple!

The first fellowships were small, self-sufficient fellowships/gatherings that had a very simple structure. They were connected to a network of traveling ministries that came by at certain times to share their gifts and equip the saints.

In Hans P. Pedersen's book, *2000 years with the Holy Spirit*, he writes:

> "The fellowships were self-sufficient, but made an ideal spiritual gathering. They related to each other, helped each other, and a range of common goals bound them together. The fellowships were especially tied together through traveling preachers who were equipped with charismatic gifts and who mourned over the

fellowship's spiritual nutrition and growth. Other leaderships were apostles, prophets, teachers, pastors, and evangelists that continued in the fellowships in shorter or longer periods. No real organization existed between the fellowships. The first Christians were not paralyzed by institutions or imprisoned in organization but let themselves be lead primarily by the Holy Spirit. Through the Holy Spirit, the fellowships were taught and edified, and upcoming happenings were told beforehand." (Hans P Pedersen, Proskrift, 1999, pg 21)

When Paul wrote his letters, he intended them to be read in the other gatherings as well.

Now when this epistle is read among you, see that it is read also in the church of the Laodiceans, and that you likewise read the epistle from Laodicea." (Col. 4:16)

So keep it simple! Start to meet, and things will start to take form afterward as the Spirit directs.

When we talk about church, we quickly forget what the purpose of the church actually is. We tend to focus more on how to *do* church than on how to make disciples as Jesus has commanded us. So let us focus on making disciples, and let Jesus build his church.

When people ask me what I think is the best way to do church, I usually say:

"Take the next six months to make disciples. Your only focus and goal must be to make disciples of Jesus. Do whatever you can to see Christians grow in their life with God and to see new people come to faith and grow in their faith. When this is your goal, it will automatically direct you in what you need to do next. When you then have done this for half a year, I believe you will look back and say to yourself: What we have done these last six months is church. Even though it might not look like what you normally associate with the church."

This is a good way to start. In the West, we tend to put too much emphasis on details, and, in that, we forget the actual purpose for what we are doing. Then all the details and doing things perfectly become goals in and of themselves. In the next chapters, we will look a bit into how to begin and how early Christians met. But keep focused; it is all about making disciples!

23

FOOD, FELLOWSHIP, AND PRAYER

And they continued steadfastly in the apostles' doctrine and fellowship, in the breaking of bread, and in prayers. (Acts 2:42)

Here we read in the book of Acts four things that the first Christians held onto tightly.

In this chapter of this book, we will look at the apostles' teachings. We read that the gatherings were something they held onto steadfastly. They were not just members who, for some time, belonged to the same congregation. No, they were a family. They gathered together daily, and they would sell their possessions in order to help each other when needed.

> *... and sold their possessions and goods, and divided them among all, as anyone had need.* (Acts 2:45)

Fellowship is important. We all have need of friends and people who are close. A bigger church does not necessarily mean that you have more friends. Actually, it is usually harder to find close friends in a large fellowship. We greet each other in the meetings, and we know each other's names, but the relationship often stays at that level. This is another reason why we need small gatherings where you can really get to know each other. Small gatherings are like small families.

They not only met in their homes in those first fellowships, they also met in the city, specifically in the area around the temple, which was like a marketplace for them. In doing so, they would meet other brothers and sisters, and together they would share Jesus Christ with the people who came by, people who did not know Him yet. They set examples there to new Christians and encouraged each other in practical ways.

Just like we have a need for small gatherings, it is important that we also meet in larger gatherings so that we realize we are part of something bigger. It is a really good idea to have relationships with other fellowships, so you can sometimes meet together as well.

We read that God added daily those who were being saved. These new converts were primarily won in the temple place and then became part of the small gatherings.

> So continuing daily with one accord in the temple, and breaking bread from house to house, they ate their food with gladness and simplicity of heart, praising God and having favor with all the people. And the Lord added to the church daily those who were being saved. (Acts 2:46-47)

Another thing that was a big part of the practice of the first fellowships was the breaking of bread. This breaking of bread was a part of the common meal time where they ate together and had fun. In the *Everyday Danish Bible*, the term "breaking of bread" has been translated with "common meal time," which is explained as follows:

> "The text here is talking about the 'breaking of bread.' It was partly a course of the common meal time amongst Christians in the home and partly a celebration of communion." (*Everyday Danish Bible*, pg. 177)

The idea of eating together is an important part of every culture. When we eat together, we get to know each other better. We relax, and the conversation can be more natural. Nothing helps a friendship grow like a good meal time.

Finally, we read that the apostles held fast to prayer. Prayer is what gets things going. Without prayer, nothing happens. Prayer is an important part of our gatherings with others and with God. The reason for this is that prayer is so intimate. When we are praying out loud, we are showing others what is on our hearts. Through this, we get to know each other well.

Some years ago, Lene and I went to a training school. There were several Russians at the school. All the Russians could speak English, but there were very few who prayed in English. When three months had gone by and the training school was over, I had experienced the importance of prayer when it comes to getting to know each other. I had developed a real relationship only with the Russians who had prayed in English. It was as if they had uncovered their hearts and their deepest desires through their prayers, desires that I could understand and relate to. This is why prayer is such an important part of a gathering. Common prayer helps us get to know each other. We get to see what is inside people, what people have on their hearts.

Prayer is also an important part of meeting with God. Prayer is not only us talking to God but God talking to us. Prayer is always supposed to be a two-way communication. In prayer, we are talking with God, seeking Him, being still before Him, and He is talking to us. Prayer changes things. There will not be any awakening without prayer. Nothing changes without prayer.

These three things, combined with the apostles' teaching (which we shall look at in the next chapter), were a big part of the first fellowships' practice. The fellowship was like a family. They ate together and shared communion, sought God together, and held fast to the teachings that the apostles came with. There was not any building, membership, or an organization that held them together.

In this chapter, I have talked about the basic building blocks for small fellowships. Of course, there are more aspects involved and each gathering will have its own identity and focus.

In some gatherings, the focus might be more on evangelism, where others focus more on fellowship and seeking God. For this reason, the traveling ministries are very important to help the gatherings to develop all different aspects in order to be strong and balanced. Every single gathering should have a focus "upward," "inward," and "outward."

Up to God, *in* to each other, and *out* to other people. For this reason, God has given the five-fold ministry to travel around and equip the fellowships in these different aspects.

24
The Apostles' Teaching

Throughout this book, I have put a strong emphasis on the importance of having the right structure for our fellowships. Having the right structure allows us to effectively make people into disciples of Jesus. However, the right structure alone is not enough to accomplish this.

I am convinced that we are standing before a third and possibly the last reformation before Jesus comes again. This reformation is mainly going to be about the structure within the fellowship. I also know that if Satan cannot stop it in one way, he is going to try in another. If he cannot stop something new from breaking through, then he will try to falsify it. He will try to create something that looks like the new thing that God is doing in order to confuse us and to create a negative attitude toward the things that are actually coming from God.

Another one of Satan's tactics is to sow confusion and doubt about what God is really saying. He does so because he knows that, without the Word of God, we will be led astray. When Satan tempted Eve in the Garden of Eden, it was with these words: "Has God really said …?" (Gen. 3:1). And when he later comes to tempt Jesus in the desert, the tactic is exactly the same. This time, however, he takes the Word out of the context in which it was written in order to make it appear that God said something that He actually has not said.

Then he brought Him to Jerusalem, set Him on the pinnacle of the temple, and said to Him, "If You are the Son of God, throw Yourself down from here. For it is written: 'He shall give His angels charge over you, to keep you,' and, 'In their hands they shall bear you up, lest you dash your foot against a stone.'" And Jesus answered and said to him, "It has been said, 'You shall not tempt the Lord your God.'" (Luke 4:9-12)

Satan is working in the same way today. He says: "Has God really said...?" He is sowing doubt and confusion about what God has said. Or, he is saying, "It is written ..." while taking the Word out of its context and, in doing so, distorting the Word of God. This is exactly what we see happening around us today.

Paul writes to the fellowship in Corinth:

For I am jealous for you with godly jealousy. For I have betrothed you to one husband, that I may present you as a chaste virgin to Christ. But I fear, lest somehow, as the serpent deceived Eve by his craftiness, so your minds may be corrupted from the simplicity that is in Christ. For if he who comes preaches another Jesus whom we have not preached, or if you receive a different spirit which you have not received, or a different gospel which you have not accepted–you may well put up with it! For I consider that I am not at all inferior to the most eminent apostles. (2 Cor. 11:2-5)

Afterward, Paul continues to talk about the false apostles. He is talking about how we must not turn away from the pure and simple devotion to Christ. It is about Jesus and about how we as His fellowship, should be a holy and pure bride. We must be on our guard for every teaching that distracts us from Jesus and our pure devotion to Him.

The Bible clearly says that, in the last days, many are going to fall away from the faith because they listen to seductive teachings (1 Tim. 4:1). This Scripture is speaking of the time in which we are now living. Therefore, it is important that we hold fast to the apostles' teaching, just like the first fellowships did. Today, we do not have the first apostles with us anymore, but what they said is written down in the Bible. The four gospels of Jesus Christ and the rest of the New Testament are what we call the apostles' teaching.

I think that Paul describes the time we are living in today really well here:

Now the Spirit expressly says that in latter times some will depart from the faith, giving heed to deceiving spirits and doctrines of demons, speaking lies in hypocrisy, having their own conscience seared with a hot iron. (1 Tim. 4:1-2)

Later, he comes with this warning to Timothy:

I charge you therefore before God and the Lord Jesus Christ, who will judge the living and the dead at His appearing and His kingdom: Preach the Word! Be ready in season and out of season. Convince, rebuke, exhort, with all longsuffering and teaching. For the time will come when they will not endure sound doctrine, but according to their own desires, because they have itching ears, they will heap up for themselves teachers; and they will turn their ears away from the truth, and be turned aside to fables. (2 Tim. 4:1-4)

We are truly living in a time when many are heaping up teachers, the ones they like to listen to, while they close their ears to the truth and to sound teaching.

Paul says later that sound teaching is the teaching that leads to the fear of God. In which churches do we hear this sound teaching that leads to the fear of God? To tell the truth, respect for a holy and righteous God is often missing in our fellowships today. Worldly thinking has slowly sneaked into many churches, even though God says that we should separate ourselves from the world so that He can receive us (2 Corinthians 6:17).

Today, we are allowing things in our lives and fellowships that God's Word says we should not accept. Many Christians are living like "the people of the world." The only difference is that they go to church on Sundays. This is not Christianity! This only shows that many who are going to churches today are not yet saved. They have yet to begin the Christian life and still need to turn away from their old life by being baptized into Christ.

Jesus came to acquire for Himself a pure and obedient people, zealous in doing good deeds (Titus 2:14). Today, we see how young people in the church are sleeping with each other before marriage and are living in fornication. We see divorce and remarriage as if it were the most normal thing in the world. All these things are, however, symptoms of an inner problem. They show that we have fallen away from true life in the power of the Holy Spirit and from the sound teaching that leads to the fear of God.

The new thing that God is doing must go together with us building on the Word of God, and us having God's Word as the highest authority in our fellowships. We can easily create a good vessel, but if what we put in it is wrong, no one should drink of it, regardless of how good the vessel is.

Notice Jesus' words about the end times:

"And because lawlessness will abound, the love of many will grow cold." (Matt. 24:12)

Did you notice that it is lawlessness, not legalism, that is going to take over? Today, some are talking so much against being legalistic that they have fallen into the ditch on the opposite side of the road into lawlessness, even when Jesus is making it clear that our biggest problem is not legalism but lawlessness. Today, an entire generation in church is living in lawlessness. They are living in sin and in rebellion against God's law, the moral law, the Ten Commandments.

God's law should be in their inner being if they have truly been born again.

"And then I will declare to them, 'I never knew you; depart from Me, you who practice lawlessness!'" (Matt. 7:23)

"You who practice lawlessness." You who are lawless and living in sin as the world does. This is what is meant by the word "lawlessness."

It is so important that we are holding fast to the apostles' teaching that we find in the Bible.

Here are some examples of what one can hear today: "Has God really said that He wants to condemn someone to hell? Has Jesus really said that the door that leads to life is small and the road narrow? Has

Jesus really said that fornicators, liars, thieves, and greedy people will not inherit God's kingdom? Has Jesus really said that we should believe in Him? Is it not about believing in yourself?"

Therefore, we must be on our guard so that we do not turn away from the simple and pure devotion to Jesus Christ and His Word. We must hold fast to the apostles' teaching. We must live in the power of the Holy Spirit as true disciples of Jesus Christ, which is what my book, *Christian, Disciple, or Slave,* is about.

If the content is not right, then the structure is totally irrelevant. God's Word should be the highest authority in our gatherings. When we are together, everything we do is based on God's Word and the apostles' teaching. Whenever we have questions, it is God's Word we must go to. A fellowship will grow in a healthy way when we take God's Word as the highest authority and give place to the work of the Holy Spirit. But whenever one of these two is missing, it will fail, regardless of how the structure looks.

25

LET THE REFORMATION BEGIN

Eight years ago, I received a prophecy from an acknowledged prophet from Sweden who has now passed away. His name is John Brandström. When I received this prophecy, I believed I knew what it was about, but I really did not at all. It is only now that I am beginning to understand it. This is the prophecy I received, and it also has to do with you:

> "A new day is coming when it will no longer be about programs or systems. I want to move My church beyond that and let it be led by my Holy Spirit. Let Me build My church by the Holy Spirit, and there will be revelations, and you are going to be one of the first who will live this."

Yes, it is becoming a new day for us all. God is truly on a journey to build His own church. Do you want to be included? Do you dare to let go of the programs and systems and let the Holy Spirit come in? Do you dare to go out with God's Word as the highest authority?

It will be the same with this book as with other books. Some are going to accept the message, and others are not going to accept it. In the gospel of Mark, chapter four, we can read about the different types of soil. There are different kinds of responses when God's Word is preached. It is going to be the same with this book. If I were to make a brief account of the message from Mark's gospel so that it reflects the message in this book, then it would look like this:

> "That which falls on the road are those who read this book but do not understand it and, therefore, cannot accept it. That which falls on the rocky ground are those who immediately accept the message in this book, but it does not take root in them, and, because of that, they fall back into the old system, forgetting what they have read. That which falls among the weeds are those who understand the message but cannot handle the consequences of leaving what is already established to go out into the new. Their environment and fear of opposition suffocate the Word so that it does not change anything in their lives. Then there are those who understand the word and accept it. They begin to take it in and to walk with greater and greater freedom as God shows them what it is all about. Afterward, they start going to a simple gathering, and they start to build simple gatherings themselves. It means that they are going to bear fruit: some thirty, some sixty, and some a hundred fold."

"What if everyone leaves the traditional church and begins simple gatherings?" you might ask. Yes, that is a good question that I really have a hard time answering. On one hand, we must respect the traditional church and the way it does things. After all, it has gotten the majority of us where we are today. On the other hand, we are in need of this radical reformation of our system. We must remember that it is the *system* that we are against, and not our brothers and sisters who exist inside the system. So, yes, we must respect people in the choice they make, but, at the same time, we must be bold and speak out. The church needs to know what God is saying in His Word and what fellowship is really meant to be. We are called to make people into disciples and not just visitors of a church.

"How is the message going to be accepted?" I am convinced that several traditional fellowships are going to accept what I have to say and are going to learn something good from it, especially if the leadership is involved. It is, after all, difficult to change such a system from the bottom up. Some will be forced to leave the system, while others will try to make a mix of it. But that is not going to work because it will be like keeping new wine in old wineskins. Hopefully, there will also be some in the traditional fellowships who will go all the way and change the whole system. Perhaps they will split up into simple, small gatherings and begin meeting regularly as a network of gatherings.

So, the truth be told, these are hard questions to answer. There is one thing I know, however, and that is that God wants to do something new. Jesus is currently building His fellowship: A pure, radiant, and holy bride ready for His return.

As Jesus is saying here, the old and new do not work together. New wine must be held in new wineskins. Then, neither the wine nor the wineskin get ruined.

> *Then He spoke a parable to them: "No one puts a piece from a new garment on an old one; otherwise the new makes a tear, and also the piece that was taken out of the new does not match the old. And no one puts new wine into old wineskins; or else the new wine will burst the wineskins and be spilled, and the wineskins will be ruined. But new wine must be put into new wineskins, and both are preserved.*
> (Luke 5:36-38)

Therefore, we need to remember to respect the "old" as well as giving place to the "new" that God wants to do. I am writing "old" and "new" within quotation marks because what I am writing about in this book actually belongs to "the old." We have simply looked at how the first fellowships were functioning. They did not have most of the things that we have associated with the church today. Everything we see around us today is something new that has come after that. However, as we can also read in the following verse, it is the "old," the original, that is the best, and when you have first tasted that, you cannot go back to the second best.

> *"And no one, having drunk old wine, immediately desires new; for he says, 'The old is better.'"* (Luke 5:39)

When you first taste what fellowship really is and experience the freedom that comes when we do things in a simple way, you will never want to go back to the "system" again. Yes, it can be hard, and it has its price, but no matter what it costs, you will not want to go back because this is the real thing. As we read, both the old and the new will be preserved, at least until the day when persecution puts a stop to it. Our traditional churches cannot run when there is persecution. So when persecution comes to us, like we see in many other countries, it will mean the end of the traditional church. When this happens, God has already built up a fellowship that can stand firm and help those people who must then come in.

Do I believe it is going to go smoothly when people begin with this reformation? No, not at all. That is what I explained in the beginning of the book. I hope, of course, that it will take place as smoothly as it can, but when people start to understand this and want to take this road, it is going to create conflicts. It is unavoidable.

I received this prophetic word some months ago:

"I see a map of Denmark, and I see that Denmark is going to be separated and torn. You must give up yourself if you are willing to pay the price."

Yes, it is something we all must do: give up ourselves because it has a cost, and it will divide us.

Where do you stand in all of this? Well, that is what time will tell. Maybe you are going to take in some of this, and maybe you are going to be one of those whom God is calling, one of those who will help in the building of His fellowship and who will pave the way for others so that even more can come into the green and fruitful land. If so, you must be willing to lay down your life in order to be able to do what needs to be done. Maybe you will begin to investigate this idea of fellowship a little more. Maybe you will start something. Or maybe you will share this with others in your fellowship. Regardless of where you stand, it is important that you seek God for yourself. If you seek God with all your heart, He is going to lead you.

I hope that this book is going to be a blessing to your life. I hope that, in one way or another, it can be part of a reformation that starts in your life.

Jesus wants to build His church with His Holy Spirit, and He wants to use you as a living stone. So, give Him permission to do it, and let the third reformation begin.

God bless you.

Torben Søndergaard
A disciple of Jesus Christ
www.TheLastReformation.com

Sound Doctrine

Teaching that leads to true fear of the Lord

Sound Doctrine is both different and prophetic. It was written out of a call from God Who gave the author the message one chapter at a time each day over a two-week period following 40 days of fasting and seeking God. It is a testimony of how the true Word of God changed the author's life and how it can also change the lives of others.

After the 40-day fast, Søndergaard was filled with new revelations from God. He felt he had to express some of the things God had given him, so he began to write. Each day over the next two weeks, God gave him another chapter. The book you are holding is the fruit of that time.

There is much misunderstanding about the "fear of the Lord." Some call it a reverent awe. Others call it a deep respect. Some believe God is just waiting for the opportunity to punish them. Some do not even consider it at all. But what is it really? What is true fear of the Lord? Torben Søndergaard's teaching on "sound doctrine" answers that question in a way that will cause Christians to honestly desire to live a more holy and pure life free from sin.

This book may be purchased in paperback from
www.TheLaurusCompany.com
and other retailers around the world. Also available in eBook format for
electronic readers from their respective stores.

OTHER BOOKS BY
TORBEN SØNDERGAARD

Christian, Disciple, or Slave

What is a Christian? The answer to this essential question today unfortunately depends on who you ask. In this book, you get the biblical answer to what a Christian really is, and how you can become a Christian. You will also be taken on a journey through the Bible as we look at various words people use for those who follow Jesus, words such as "Christian," "disciple," and "slave."

Many of us have heard the expression: "I am a Christian, but in my own way," or "I am a Christian, but am not so much into it." But is it even possible to be a Christian in one's own personal way? The author argues that, according to the Bible, the answer is no, just as it is not possible to be a disciple or a slave in one's own personal way.

The book is written for both Christian and non-Christian. A radical book, it takes a hard look at what Jesus Himself said about being a Christian. Jesus' words are extremely radical, but it is the place where we get the true answer to the question: "What is a real Christian?"

This book may be purchased in paperback from
www.TheLaurusCompany.com
and other retailers around the world. Also available in eBook format for
electronic readers from their respective stores.

OTHER PUBLICATIONS BY
TORBEN SØNDERGAARD

"Life as a Christian"

"Complete the Race"

"Deceived?" (Booklet)

"The Twisted Race" (Booklet

These Publications can be found on the author's website at:

www.TheLastReformation.com

ABOUT THE AUTHOR

Torben Søndergaard

Torben Søndergaard lives in Denmark in the city of Herning with his wife, Lene, and their three children.

Torben grew up in a non-Christian family. On April 5, 1995, after attending a church service with a friend, he turned to God and had a strong, personal encounter with Jesus that totally changed his life. Five years later, from a Scripture in the Bible and in a sort of desperation after more of God, Torben started on a 40-day fast that transformed many things in his life. His eyes were more open to God's Word and what the gospel is about. He began to understand how lukewarm and far away from the truth Christians had become. He saw that God had called him to speak His Word without compromise.

Torben has seen many people saved, healed, and set free from demons. He has written seven books and is the founder of the mission organization, Experience Jesus. He is known for having a direct approach to the Bible and for his personal life with God. Many know him from national Danish TV, where he has appeared many times, or they know him from his videos on YouTube.com. You can read more on his website: www.TheLastReformation.com

CPSIA information can be obtained
at www.ICGtesting.com
Printed in the USA
LVOW05s0049130117

520803LV00010B/56/P